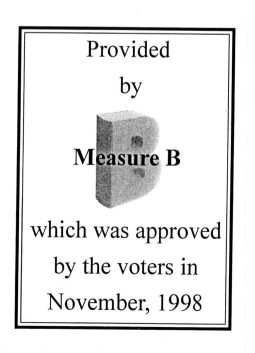

Aquatic
Life
of the World

Volume 1
Abalone–Barracuda

Marshall Cavendish Corporation
99 White Plains Road
Tarrytown, New York 10591–9001

Library of Congress Cataloging-in-Publication Data
Aquatic life of the world.
    p.   cm.
    Contents: v. 1. Abalone–Barracuda — v. 2. Bass–Conservation — v. 3. Continental shelf–Fiddler crab — v. 4. Fin whale–Hydrothermal vent — v. 5. Iceberg–Manatee and dugong — v. 6. Mangrove–Ocean history — v. 7. Oceanography–Puffin — v. 8. Remora–Sea otter — v. 9. Sea pen–Swordfish — v. 10. Tarpon–Wrasse — v. 11. Index.
    ISBN 0-7614-7170-7 (set) — ISBN 0-7614-7171-5 (v. 1) — ISBN 0-7614-7172-3 (v. 2) — ISBN 0-7614-7173-1 (v. 3) — ISBN 0-7614-7174-X (v. 4) — ISBN 0-7614-7175-8 (v. 5) — ISBN 0-7614-7176-6 (v. 6) — ISBN 0-7614-7177-4 (v. 7) — ISBN 0-7614-7178-2 (v. 8) — ISBN 0-7614-7179-0 (v. 9) — ISBN 0-7614-7180-4 (v. 10) — ISBN 0-7614-7181-2 (index)
    1. Aquatic biology—Juvenile literature. [1. Aquatic biology—Encyclopedias. 2. Marine animals—Encyclopedias. 3. Freshwater animals—Encyclopedias.] I. Marshall Cavendish Corporation.

QH90.16.A78 2000
578.76—dc21

99-086128

ISBN 0-7614-7170-7 (set)
ISBN 0-7614-7171-5 (volume 1)

Printed in Hong Kong

06 05 04 03 02 01 6 5 4 3 2 1

Brown Partworks
Project editor: Bridget Giles
Subeditors: Amanda Harman, Tim Harris, Tom Jackson, James Kinchen, Jane Scarsbrook, Jens Thomas
Managing editor: Anne O'Daly
Designer: Alison Gardner
Picture researchers: Veneta Bullen, Helen Simm
Illustrator: Christopher Jory
Graphics: Mark Walker
Indexer: Kay Ollerenshaw

Marshall Cavendish Corporation
Editor: Marian Armstrong
Editorial director: Paul Bernabeo

WRITERS

Richard Beatty
Dylan Bright
Jen Green
James Kinchen
Dr. Robbie A. MacDonald
Samantha Rohr

Paul L. Sieswerda
Dr. Sergio Steffani
Dr. Robert Stewart
Dr. Robert Stickney
Dr. Laurence G. Riddle
Brian Ward

SET CONTENTS

INTRODUCTION

Organisms, including plants, algae, animals, and bacteria, that spend all or part of their lives in or on water are aquatic. This includes those that inhabit a puddle as well as those that live in rivers, lakes, oceans, and seas. *Aquatic Life of the World* reveals the creatures and habitats of the Earth's underwater realms. From the smallest pond to the deepest ocean trench, life abounds, and this 11-volume set covers all the major aquatic life-forms as well as many of the little-known rarer ones.

EXTREME HABITATS

Aquatic habitats are among the most challenging on Earth. They range from below-freezing polar oceans to boiling-hot thermal waters, many with strong currents that relentlessly batter organisms. Some aquatic habitats disappear for whole seasons or years when they evaporate during dry periods, leaving their inhabitants stranded. The beach is a particularly extreme place to live: every day it is flooded by salty water, struck by powerful waves, and then left exposed to the Sun.

Elsewhere, sunlight only penetrates surface waters. In some muddy rivers and deep waters it can be impossible to see more than a few feet in any direction. Deep in the oceans a wide range of animals live in complete darkness, some emitting a glow to light their way, attract prey, or repel predators. The

▼ **Water is the most abundant substance on Earth. Most of the roughly 326 million cubic miles (1.4 billion cubic km) of water is held in the ocean; the rest is in rivers, lakes, glaciers, groundwaters, and in the air (as water vapor, which forms clouds). Water vapor condenses into rain and cycles back to the air as vapor via evaporation and transpiration.**

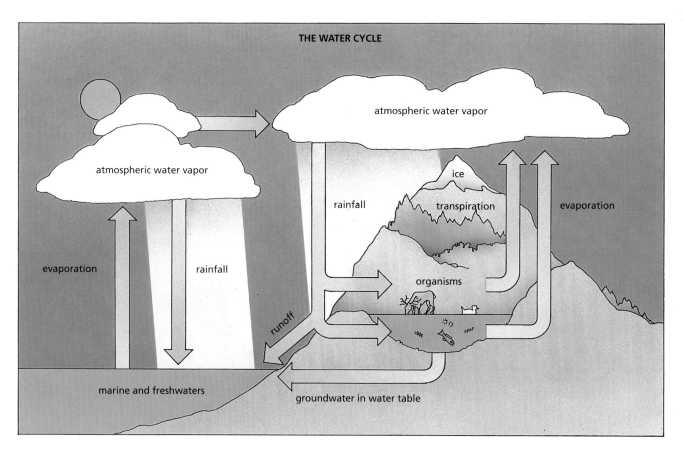

THE WATER CYCLE

atmospheric water vapor

atmospheric water vapor

rainfall

ice

transpiration

evaporation

evaporation

rainfall

organisms

runoff

marine and freshwaters

groundwater in water table

open ocean is a daunting place to live, with little cover to hide from hungry predators and perhaps a long journey to find food or mates.

BIOLOGICAL DIVERSITY

Despite the harsh conditions in watery habitats, the variety of life there far exceeds that on land. Organisms have adapted in a myriad of ways to the conditions, resulting in great biological diversity. Life probably first evolved in the oceans, and the march of evolution can still be traced in today's species, some of which have changed little from their ancestors of millions of years ago—hagfish and lampreys, for example. The ancestors of whales and dolphins, however, were land-dwelling mammals that returned to the sea. Over millions of years they evolved to look more like fish than their closer relatives, such as humans, cats, and dogs.

Some animals, especially many fish, spend their whole lives in water and are unable to exist outside of their aquatic habitat. Animals from turtles and crocodiles to seals and walruses spend most of their time in the water but emerge to breed on land. Even some fish, such as the mudskipper, can leave their watery homes long enough to travel across land or even climb trees, while lungfish bury themselves in the mud to wait out the dry season. Many birds actively seek out prey underwater, diving to amazing depths to catch their meals.

Other animals spend only part of their life cycle in water. The young of insects often live and feed in freshwater habitats, then change their form completely to become winged adults that are as at home in the air as they once were in the water. Salamanders and newts have a variety of complex life cycles. Some spend their adult lives on land, returning to ponds to breed, while others spend their whole lives in water or emerge to live on land for only a few years as bright red efts.

This diversity is also reflected in how aquatic organisms breed, breathe, feed, and move about. For example, with many fish and invertebrates, reproduction involves simply releasing eggs and sperm into the water for fertilization; other animals take great care of their young, protecting them from predators and teaching them survival skills.

LOOKING TO THE FUTURE

Every year scientists discover new aquatic species. Parts of the ocean that were once as difficult to get to as the Moon have now been visited, albeit rarely. As technology improves and scientific knowledge grows, it is likely that even more of Earth's underwater secrets will be revealed. ◆

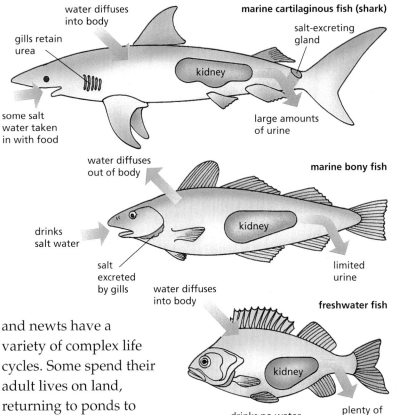

marine cartilaginous fish (shark)

water diffuses into body

gills retain urea

salt-excreting gland

kidney

some salt water taken in with food

large amounts of urine

water diffuses out of body

marine bony fish

drinks salt water

kidney

salt excreted by gills

limited urine

water diffuses into body

freshwater fish

kidney

drinks no water

plenty of urine

▲ **Aquatic animals have to control the levels of water inside their bodies. Marine fish drink salt water, but excess salt will lead to dehydration. By excreting salt and retaining urea (a waste chemical), sharks draw water into the body. To prevent dehydration, bony fish produce small amounts of urine, and the gills remove salt. To stop too much water flooding freshwater fish, none is drunk and large amounts are excreted as urine.**

READER'S GUIDE

color-coded running head   title

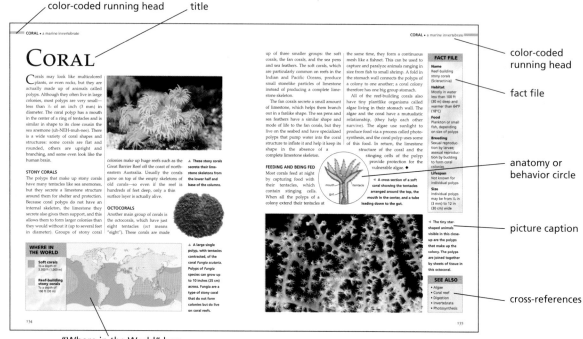

color-coded running head

fact file

anatomy or behavior circle

picture caption

cross-references

"Where in the World" box

These pages explain how to use *Aquatic Life of the World*. There are more than 200 alphabetically arranged articles in the set. To find articles on a particular subject or organism, use the set contents list that appears in this volume. If it is not listed there, try looking it up in the index volume, volume 11, which includes a comprehensive index for the whole set as well as several subject indexes. Each volume has its own contents list and index, and at the back of each volume a glossary explains important terms.

Every article is lavishly illustrated with color photographs and artworks. Articles cover a range of topics, from how specific aquatic organisms live, feed, and reproduce to more general subjects such as conservation, digestion, and locomotion. Some entries are about only one species. The humpback whale,

for instance, has its own article. Other articles discuss more than one species. *Catfish*, for example, explores the distinctive traits these fish share while also introducing readers to the diversity of catfish forms and lifestyles.

Even larger groups of related organisms are discussed in entries such as *mollusk*, *mammal*, *crustacean*, and *insect*. How organisms are arranged into different families and groups by scientists is explained in greater detail in volume 11. Family trees in that volume explain which organisms covered in *Aquatic Life of the World* are related to each other and how they are classified. The comprehensive index in volume 11 can also be used to look up organisms by group, family, or type. "See Also" boxes within each article provide cross-references that guide readers to related articles elsewhere in the set.

"WHERE IN THE WORLD"

Most species are found only in certain parts of the world. They might live in the freezing polar waters or in warm tropical seas. "Where in the World" boxes illustrate where particular species or groups of related species live. Readers will be able to tell at a glance whether an animal is coastal, lives in the open sea, or is only found in one river or lake.

Species are not always found throughout the ranges shown. Entire land-masses may be colored in for freshwater fish, for example, though they are only found in lakes and rivers. Also, many marine creatures are only found at certain depths. Check the map key for extra information.

Ranges shown are those correct at the time of publication. If a certain part of the world's marine or freshwaters are not colored in, this does not necessarily mean that the organism does not live there but perhaps that it has not yet been found there. Estimating the range of marine organisms can be very difficult, and for many species only limited information exists.

FACT FILES

Every article has one or more fact files. In articles on individual species or limited groups of related species, fact files provide information on a species' habitat, what it eats, how it reproduces, how long it lives, and how big it can get. Fact files also include the scientific names and the common names of organisms. Sometimes organisms have no common name, so only a scientific name is given. (See volume 11 for more on this.) In articles that cover larger groups of organisms or more general topics, fact files summarize points made in the text and give concise definitions of key terms. Fact files in habitat articles list the type of organisms found and what threats exist.

ANATOMY AND BEHAVIOR CIRCLES

Artworks inside circles (or ovals) depict aspects of an organism's anatomy or behavior. To find out what a sea gooseberry's feeding tentacle looks like, for example, check out the anatomy circle in *comb jelly*. Or, to find out how some fish keep their babies in their mouth, see the behavior circle in *cichlid*. ◆

◄ Examples of two anatomy circles, showing the extendable lower lip of a dragonfly nymph (top) and the underside of a chiton.

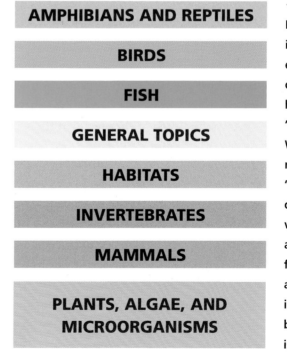

AMPHIBIANS AND REPTILES

BIRDS

FISH

GENERAL TOPICS

HABITATS

INVERTEBRATES

MAMMALS

PLANTS, ALGAE, AND MICROORGANISMS

◄ COLOR CODES: Each article falls into one of the eight color-coded categories shown here. Fact files, "Where in the World" boxes, running heads, and "See Also" boxes are colored to reflect which category the article falls into. So, for example, the article *marine iguana* is color coded orange because this animal is a reptile.

ABALONE

◀ An abalone uses
its muscular foot to
cling tightly to rocks.
Tentacles on the
abalone's head and
around the edge of
its mantle are used
to locate food.

FACT FILE

Name
Red abalone
(*Haliotis rufescens*)

Distinctive features
Broad, flat, brick-red shell; row of holes at front

Habitat
Rocky seashore and kelp forests off California

Behavior
Mostly anchored to rocks but can move slowly

Food
Algae, especially seaweed

Breeding
Eggs and sperm released into water, where fertilization occurs; larvae float in plankton before settling on seabed

Lifespan
Up to 15 years

Size
Up to 12 in (30 cm) across

Few shellfish are more highly prized by people than abalones. Their flesh is used as food, while their shells can be polished and made into jewelry. These large mollusks are found on seashores and in shallow coastal waters in many parts of the world, wherever there is warm water, a rocky bottom, and plenty of their favorite food—seaweed. In these areas human divers compete with natural predators such as sea otters and bat rays to gather abalones.

SHELL DWELLERS

Abalones are part of a group of mollusks called gastropods. Like other members of this group, such as snails, abalones have a coiled shell to protect their bodies. An abalone's shell is wide and flat and acts like a shield over its back. The ridged outer surface of the shell is usually encrusted with algae and blends perfectly with the surrounding rocks. This camouflage helps to protect the abalone from predators.

Beneath its shell, the abalone has a simple body. It clings to and crawls across rocks using a large muscle called a foot. Around the foot is a ring of tentacles that allows the abalone to detect chemicals in the seawater. It can also see light and dark with the pair of simple eyes attached to its head.

LIFE CYCLES

Abalones breed by releasing their eggs or sperm into the water through the holes in their shell. There, sperm from the males fertilize eggs from the females. The fertilized eggs develop into larvae, which float in the plankton. After about a week the larvae sink to the bottom and begin to develop into adults. It will be two years before they will be developed enough to breed.

Only a tiny proportion of the larvae survive to maturity. Many are swept away on ocean currents or dashed against rocks, and large numbers of juveniles are eaten by predators such as starfish, crabs, and fish. To compensate for these losses, abalones produce an enormous number of eggs: 11 million from a single 8-inch (20-cm) female. To improve their chances of survival, small abalones shelter in rock crevices or among the spines of sea urchins during the day, emerging at night to feed. Full-grown abalones have fewer enemies and like to occupy open positions, where there is more food.

DECLINING NUMBERS

People in many parts of the world harvest abalones. The largest species, the red abalone, is collected along the coast of California, while in southern Australia divers pursue the smaller Roe's abalone. As the demand for abalones has increased, the stocks of these and several other species have declined significantly, arousing fears that the populations may be wiped out

by overfishing. Strict laws limiting catch sizes have been introduced, but abalone numbers have been slow to recover. A more successful approach has been to rear abalones in captivity and then release them in areas where wild populations have declined. ◆

▲ The richly colored inside of an abalone's shell is secreted by the mantle. This nacre is used to make costume jewelry.

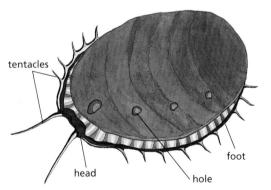

tentacles

head

hole

foot

◀ Abalones, such as this red abalone, breathe by allowing water to pass under the front edge of the shell, over the internal gills, then out of holes at the front of the shell. Sperm or eggs and wastes are released through these holes.

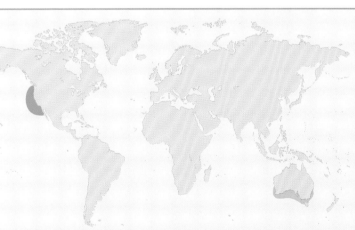

WHERE IN THE WORLD

Red abalone
From tidal zone to a depth of 100 ft (30 m)

Roe's abalone
From tidal zone to a depth of 15 ft (5 m)

SEE ALSO

• Invertebrate
• Mollusk
• Snail

ALGAE

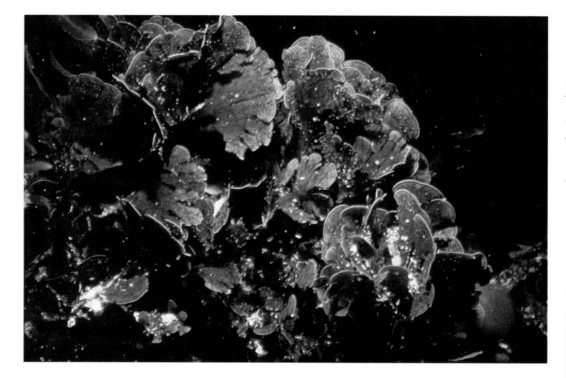

FACT FILE

Microalgae
Microscopic organisms that are found everywhere; they are most common in aquatic habitats and are the base of nearly all aquatic food webs

Diatoms
Yellow to brown marine and freshwater algae

Dinoflagellates
Mostly marine yellowish-brown algae. From 5 to 2,000 micrometers (µm)

Euglenoids
Brackish and freshwater algae from 15 to 500 µm

Unicellular green algae
Microscopic freshwater forms, including volvox

Algae can be microscopic single cells that are invisible to the naked eye or large multicellular organisms such as seaweeds. Although large algae are usually considered plants, recent reclassifications of some smaller single-celled species are now placed between plants and animals in the protist kingdom, along with amoebas and slime molds.

Like plants, algae convert the Sun's rays to energy via a process called photosynthesis. Most algae perform this using tiny structures (organelles) inside their cells called chloroplasts, which contain the green pigment chlorophyll, as well as pigments of other colors. Some algae steal photosynthetic organelles from other algae. Unlike plants, though, algae do not have roots, stems, or leaves. Several microscopic algae have whiplike flagella that they lash in the water to move, but most simply drift in surface waters. Seaweeds anchor to rocks by holdfasts.

LIFE-GIVING ALGAE

Algae live in salt water and freshwater all over the planet. They can occur in and on soils and on moist stones and wood; they might also be found living in partnership with animals such as hydras, marine worms, coral polyps, sea anemones, and jellyfish.

Algae form the base of most marine and freshwater food chains. Phytoplankton (diatoms, dinoflagellates, and single-celled green algae) are filtered from the water by zooplankton (tiny animal-like organisms) and fish such as the ocean sunfish and sardines. These in turn are eaten by larger animals. In marine habitats there are few flowering plants, so algae ultimately maintain all life in the oceans. Phytoplankton photo-synthesize during the day, absorbing carbon dioxide and nutrients and releasing oxygen as a byproduct. These microscopic protists are credited with the formation of Earth's atmosphere, the protective ozone layer, and nearly half the oxygen we breathe.

Many algae are also economically important to people, as food or for use in the manufacture of other products. More than 70 species of seaweeds are eaten. *Porphyra*, a red alga also called nori, is farmed in bays and shallow seas in many parts of Asia. Some green algae are used as supplements in homeo-pathic medicine. Crude oil and natural gas are the remnants of ancient algae.

ALGAL DIVERSITY
Algae can be divided into single-celled or tiny microalgae and multicellular macroalgae. Microalgae includes eugle-noids, dinoflagellates, golden algae (chrysophytes), and diatoms. Macro-algae includes green algae, brown algae, and red algae, though green and red algae can be single- or multicelled. (Blue-green algae are a type of bacteria more correctly called cyanobacteria.)

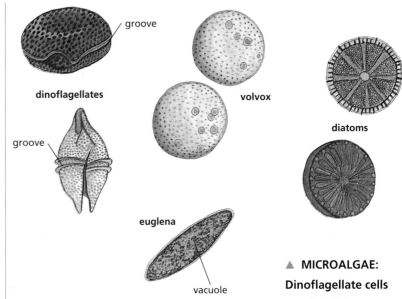

dinoflagellates

groove

volvox

diatoms

euglena

vacuole

EUGLENOIDS
There are 800 species of euglenoids, most of which consist of just a single cell. These species are considered to be ancient, primitive organisms, possibly among the first forms of life on Earth.

DINOFLAGELLATES
Dinoflagellates are mostly single celled, but they possess two flagellae, which allow them to move. High reproduction rates lead to blooms (huge concentra-tions) of dinoflagellates. Blooms can color the water brown, yellow, or red.

▲ **MICROALGAE:**
Dinoflagellate cells are circled by a groove that contains one of their two flagellae. Euglena species absorb food across the cell surface and digest it within vacuoles or produce food by photosynthesis. Diatoms are either free floating, attached to hard surfaces, or buried in sand. Volvox are oval hollow colonies the size of a pinhead that contain up to 60,000 algal cells. Most of these microalgae repro-duce by cell division, but a few reproduce sexually. Small daughter colonies develop from sperm and eggs inside the volvox capsules, for instance.

WHERE IN THE WORLD

Porphyra
Shallow waters

Sea lettuce
Intertidal zone

The term *red tide* refers to certain types of dinoflagellate blooms; these can harm marine life. Some dinoflagellates, and also a few diatoms, release toxins that are harmful to fish, shellfish, marine mammals, and even humans.

Some dinoflagellates, known as zooanthellae, live in partnership with reef-building corals. The algal cells live inside the coral polyp's body, supplying it with oxygen and food (carbohydrates), while the coral animal provides a stable environment and a source of carbon dioxide and nutrients. Since the relationship benefits both partners, it is termed mutualism.

DIATOMS

The diatoms are mostly single-celled algae with golden brown or yellow-green pigments. Many have highly ornate glassy cell walls made of silica. Diatoms contain oil that aids flotation. They live singly or in long colonies. Some elongated diatoms move around by sliding along hard surfaces or each other. Diatomite is a marine deposit formed by huge quantities of accumulated diatom cells. It is used for filters, insulators, and mild abrasives. Diatoms are also responsible for deposits of marine petroleum: over millions of years their tiny droplets of oil have been squeezed into porous rock and buried under layers of sediments.

GREEN ALGAE

Green algae are probably the direct ancestors of complex plants. Most live on land or in freshwater; only about 10 percent are marine. On beaches, the threadlike mermaids' hair seen on rocks and pilings and the bright green sea lettuce washed ashore are among the most noticeable forms.

In shallow tropical waters, underwater grass meadows are dotted with calcium-containing green algae shaped like shaving brushes or small green balloons. In freshwater lakes, blooms of single-celled green algae color the water in spring and fall.

◄ When too many nutrients such as nitrogen and phosphorus enter lakes (in runoff from farmland, for example), dense blooms of algae can form. These cover the water's surface, preventing sunlight from reaching underwater plants and using up much of the oxygen in the water. This process is called eutrophication.

◀ When sea temperatures rise, algae that live in corals, feeding them and giving them their color, die and are cast out. Coral "bleaching" could become more serious as Earth gets warmer through global warming.

SEE ALSO
- Coral
- Coral reef
- Kelp
- Kelp forest
- Photosynthesis
- Plankton
- Seaweed

BROWN ALGAE

There are more than 1,500 species of brown algae, and nearly all of them are marine. They dominate rocky shorelines in temperate and polar regions. Most brown algae are macroalgae. Some species of kelp, such as giant kelp, are more than 120 ft (36 m) long.

The main body of a kelp comprises many cells held together in a gel-like material called algin. Algin from kelp is used to make textiles, plastics, and ice cream. Huge mats of the floating brown algae called sargassum cover more than an acre of offshore water in the Atlantic Ocean. These mats are home to tiny camouflaged fish, shrimp, and crabs, which provide food for dolphin fish, sea turtles, and larvae.

RED ALGAE

Red algae belong to a diverse group, with more than 3,500 mostly marine species. This group contains both micro- and macroalgae. The red coloring is due to photosynthetic pigments that allow the algae to absorb the light penetrating into deeper water. They are often found deep in the water, where there is little light but plenty of space on the rocks. One rocky intertidal red algae is Irish moss, which is harvested for a substance called carrageenan. This is used to thicken and stabilize foods such as dairy products and nondairy creamers. ◆

▼ Green, red, and brown algae on a reef provide additional habitat for reef-dwelling animals. Some algae support the growth of atoll islands.

ALLIGATOR

◀ An American alligator basks on a log in the Everglades. Like other reptiles, alligators are cold-blooded, so they warm up by basking in the Sun or huddling together. To cool down, they slip into the water.

FACT FILE

Name
American alligator (*Alligator mississippiensis*)

Distinctive features
Adults gray and dark olive; fourth tooth not visible when mouth shut

Habitat
Swamps, creeks, lakes, and ponds

Behavior
Aggressive predator

Food
Insects, fish, birds, and mammals

Breeding
Female lays 20-70 eggs

Lifespan
50 to 60 years

Size
Up to 19 ft (5.8 m) long and 550 lbs (250 kg) or more

Alligators are large, semiaquatic reptiles that spend most of their lives in or near bodies of water. Modern alligators have been around for more than 65 million years. They are members of the order Crocodylia, which also includes crocodiles. Although similar, alligators and crocodiles differ in looks and habitat. Alligators can be characterized by their rounded snouts, whereas crocodiles have thinner snouts. The alligator's lower fourth tooth is not visible when the mouth is closed, while this tooth is visible in crocodiles.

TYPES OF ALLIGATORS

The Chinese alligator and the more familiar American alligator are the two alligator species found today. The five species of caimans belong to the same family as alligators. The American alligator is the largest reptile in North America, ranging in size from 6 to 19 feet (1.8 to 5.8 m) in length. Males can reach a weight of 550 pounds (250 kg) or more, while females tend to be smaller and lighter. Their long muscular tails and webbed feet make them excellent swimmers. American alligators live in tropical freshwater bayous, lakes, rivers, and swamps in the southeastern United States. Their range stretches from North Carolina to Florida and west to Texas.

The Chinese alligator is found in the Yangtze River Valley. Smaller than the American alligator, it has a similar lifestyle but eats mostly shellfish.

BREEDING

After mating in spring, female American alligators construct large mounds of vegetation and mud where they lay their eggs. Sunlight as well as warmth from the rotting vegetation incubates the eggs. A typical clutch contains between 20 and 70 eggs. The female guards her nest from predators. After approximately 60 days the eggs hatch. The female then carries the babies down to the water in her mouth. The young alligators remain close to the mother until the following spring.

LIFESTYLE AND HABITATS

Alligators are the only crocodilians that can tolerate cold. American alligators do not hibernate but remain in the water, bury themselves in mud, or enter deep holes they have dug. They can even survive frozen conditions by keeping a small hole open in the ice for breathing.

Alligators are fierce predators. Prey is captured in the jaws and taken underwater to be drowned. Alligators are not able to chew, so smaller prey animals are swallowed whole. Very large prey, such as deer, is torn into smaller pieces before being swallowed. Young alligators eat insects, frogs, fish, and other small animals. As they grow their diet broadens to include turtles, snakes, birds, larger fish, and mammals. Dead animals (carrion) are also eaten.

Due to massive hunting, poaching, and habitat loss, American alligator populations declined until 1967, when the animals were placed on the U.S. endangered species list. Conservation, captive breeding, and reduced hunting have helped this species make a comeback. Although American alligators are no longer endangered, they are still protected by law. The Chinese alligator has not been so fortunate. It is now close to extinction due to habitat loss and poaching. ◆

▲ Fewer than 1,000 Chinese alligators live in the wild. Much of their habitat has been lost due to the building of dams and draining of land.

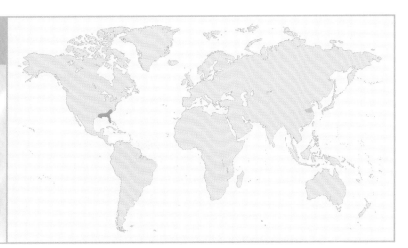

WHERE IN THE WORLD

■ **American alligator**
Swamps, lakes, and creeks

■ **Chinese alligator**
Lower Yangtze River Valley, China

▲ A female American alligator is a protective mother; she carries her young in her mouth when they are very small.

SEE ALSO

• Conservation
• Crocodile
• Reptile

AMAZON RIVER

While the Amazon River is second in length to the Nile River in Egypt, it can easily claim the title the Greatest River on Earth. The Amazon crosses South America almost at its widest point, beginning only 100 miles (160 km) from the Pacific Ocean, in the Andes Mountains of Peru. It starts its journey eastward in the Apurímac River, 17,200 feet (5,240 m) above sea level. When it discharges into the Atlantic Ocean, the waters will have traveled 4,000 miles (6,400 km)—a distance as great as that from New York

to Rome. Although it is not the longest river in the world, in volume the Amazon has no rival. It carries more water than the Mississippi, the Nile, and the Yangtze Rivers all together. In fact it is 10 times as large as the Mississippi and accounts for one-fifth of all the freshwater that runs into the world's oceans. In some places the river is wider than 6 miles (10 km), and a person standing on one side would not be able to see the opposite bank. Its average depth is 40 feet (12 m) but in some areas reaches 300 feet (90 m). So much fresh-

▲ More than 1,000 tributaries join the Amazon, creating a network of water- ways and wetlands that crisscross the Amazon basin. Many of these tributaries are major rivers in their own right. The Madeira River, for example, is more than 2,000 miles (3,200 km) long.

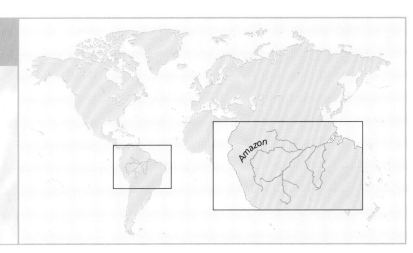

WHERE IN THE WORLD

Amazon River

Length
4,000 miles (6,400 km)

Width
Mostly 1.5 to 6 miles
(2.5 to 10 km); 90 miles
(150 km) wide at mouth

Depth
Up to 300 ft (90 m)

FACT FILE

Amazon River
World's largest
river by volume

Climate
Warm, rainy, and
humid. Average
daily temperature
in September
89°F (32°C); 75°F
(24°C) in April.
Rainfall in
lowlands from 60
to 120 in (1,500
to 3,000 mm)

Habitats
Basin has the
world's largest
rain forest. Along
the river itself:
flooded forests,
sandbanks, and
marshlands

Threats
Erosion and
habitat loss due
to logging, road
building, and
other develop-
ments; dams;
pollution; water
buffalo intro-
duced from Asia

water flows into the ocean that it dilutes the salty water for more than 100 miles (160 km) offshore.

LAND OF THE AMAZONS?

Spanish explorer Francisco de Orellana reported being attacked by fierce female warriors in 1542 when he was the first to travel the Amazon River all the way to the Atlantic. A Greek myth told of women warriors who could each fight more fiercely than 10 men and fought naked with bows and arrows. Amazons were thought to rule the surrounding tribes but lived without men in their villages. Orellana told of such warriors on this new river and that he felt lucky to have escaped with his life. This tale was told enough times to give the name Amazon to the river and its entire surroundings. No tribe of Amazons was ever discovered, but the myth is also remembered in the name that the Spanish used temporarily: *Orellana*, for its discoverer. Native South Americans called the river *Amaru-Mayu*, meaning "Great Serpent, Mother of Men."

ORIGINS

The Amazon consists of a great drainage basin almost as large as the area of the United States. The Amazon

◀ The matamata has nostrils at the tip of its long snout, which it uses like a snorkel. As the turtle lies still on the Amazon riverbed, its shell looks like a crumpled dead leaf. When a fish comes within range, the turtle opens its mouth, and water rushes in, delivering the prey.

basin is the remnant of an inland sea that covered much of the continent 5.3 to 1.6 million years ago. The sea broke into the Atlantic Ocean and drained the land into what has become the Amazon River and its surrounding rain forest. After falling steeply from the eastern slopes of the Andes, the Amazon continues on a gentle slope for most of its long course to the other side of the continent. It drops only 3 inches per mile (12 cm/km) for thousands of miles.

FLOODED FOREST

About 85 inches (2,160 mm) of rain falls throughout much of the Amazon each year. In some places this may be more than 100 inches (2,500 mm) per year. The Amazonian year is divided into rainy and dry seasons, and the water level in the river rises and falls considerably. In some areas during the rainy season, the river may rise 50 feet (15 m), overflowing its banks to inundate the rain forest. This flooding is part of the natural cycle of the Amazon ecosystem. During this time many fish, such as a vegetarian relative of the piranha called the pacu, eat fruit from overhanging plants, which are usually high and dry in the jungle. These fish fill a similar ecological

▲ Changes in surface tension of the water attract the pacu to floating fruit, seeds, and leaves upon which to feed.

◄ This flooded Amazonian forest is known as an *igapo*. Floods deposit layers of nutrient-rich silt on the forest floor and open up new feeding opportunities for fish and other animals.

SEE ALSO
- Arapaima
- Cichlid
- Flooding
- Manatee and dugong
- Otter
- River and stream
- River dolphin

niche to birds in a forest. They eat the fruit and pass the seeds as they move about. This spreads seeds around the forest, often to places where they can grow after the river recedes. Many fish migrate into the flooded forest during the rainy season and back into the main river channel during the dry season.

LIFE IN THE RIVER

The waters of the Amazon, like the rain forest around them, make up one of the world's most diverse habitats. Pink dolphins and giant river otters play in the cloudy waters. More than 1,500 species of fish are known to live in the river, and many species are yet to be identified. One of the world's largest freshwater fish, the arapaima, can still be found in the waters of the Amazon, but it is threatened with extinction.

Air travel has provided access to some of the most remote areas of the river, leading to an increase in the commercial exploitation of species. Tropical fish are now supplied to home aquariums around the world. Neon tetras, freshwater angelfish, and other brilliantly colored aquarium fish are caught and shipped to suppliers for distribution. Fortunately, many of these species are now raised on fish farms, and the loss to the river is not as great as it once was.

The threat to the remaining species comes largely from the development of towns and industries, which is taking place as the area's human population spreads up the banks of the river and into the rain forest.

ONE OF THE LAST FRONTIERS

Wild places are still to be found along the Amazon River and its many tributaries. One danger that still faces even modern-day explorers is the piranha. The threat posed to people by this fish may have been exaggerated through movies and other popular media, but piranhas are equipped with strong jaws and sharp teeth that can seriously damage large animals. The risk is greatest during the dry season in shallow water, where few other prey are available. Even humans must be careful when crossing a stream during such times. Another danger is the freshwater stingray, which can inflict a venomous sting if stepped on. In some parts of South America these fish are more feared than piranhas. ◆

▼ **The Amazon river dolphin, or boto, is most common in rough water at the junctions of rivers and tributaries. In the dry season it is confined to the major rivers, but in the rainy part of the year it enters the flooded forest, swimming among the trees. Its body color is highly variable according to age, water clarity, temperature, and location, but the young never show the pink hues of many adults.**

FACT FILE

Organisms found
Thousands of different species live in the Amazon River, some of which are: alligators; anacondas; black caimans; capybaras; aquatic herbs and grasses; fish, including arapaima, catfish and giant catfish, cichlids, lungfish, pacu, piranhas, tambaqui, and tetras; giant river otters; manatees; mosquitoes; nutria (coypu); poison arrow frogs; river dolphins; river turtles, including giant river turtles; trees that are able to stand in water, such as figs, kapuk, palms, and viriola; water buffalo

AMOEBA

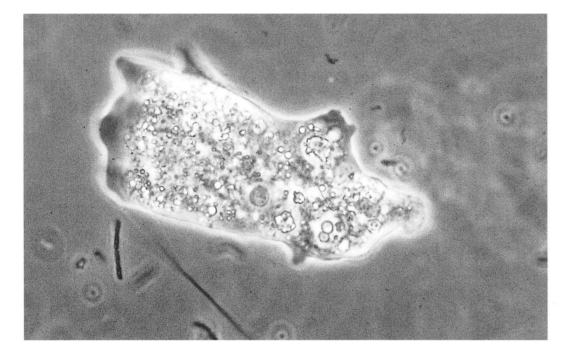

◁ An amoeba, shown here 3,500 times larger than life, extends a pseudopod to the right to move in that direction. Some amoebas make only one pseudopod, or false foot, at a time, while others will have many.

FACT FILE

Name
Amoeba species

Distinctive features
Tiny, single-celled organisms that can generate pseudopod(s)

Habitat
Freshwater, seawater, damp soil; also as parasites in animals and plants

Behavior
Can change form, but the shapes adopted depend on the species

Food
Bacteria, algae, other protozoans

Breeding
Asexual: splits into two (binary fission)

Size
About $\frac{1}{1000}$ in (0.025 mm) across

Most living organisms are made of hundreds or millions of separate cells, all working together to support the whole plant, animal, or fungus. However there are organisms, such as amoebas and bacteria, that have all their life functions contained in a single, usually microscopic, cell. Some members of the kingdom Protista are called protozoans, and they can move around and eat other organisms. Therefore, they were once considered to be animals. Other protozoans are more plantlike in character, such as the unicellular algae of the plankton.

COMMON PROTOZOANS

Protozoans can be split into several groups, with amoebas being the best-known members of the group called Sarcondina. Like other Sarcondina organisms, amoebas live mainly in water. They also live in damp soil and sediments on the seafloor and exist as parasites in animals and plants. Amoebas are very small organisms, most measuring approximately $\frac{1}{1000}$ inch (0.025 mm) in diameter. However, they are large enough to be seen with an ordinary light microscope, and samples of freshwater taken from ponds, ditches, or the beach may well contain large numbers of these creatures.

An amoeba looks like a blob of colorless gel with dark specks in it. This gel, called cytoplasm, is of two types. One type, called ectoplasm, is stiff but flexible and acts as a membrane that holds the cell together. The other type, called endoplasm, is more watery. Contained in the endoplasm are tiny structures that hold the cell's DNA and perform other essential functions. Amoebas reproduce asexually by splitting into two halves.

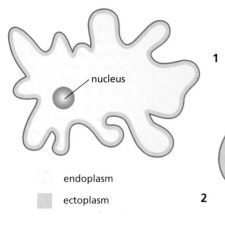

1

nucleus

endoplasm

ectoplasm

2

◄ While an amoeba is stationary (1), stiff ectoplasm borders the cell edge, surrounding the more fluid endoplasm. To move, the amoeba forms a small projection of ectoplasm called a cap (2). Endoplasm flows into this, forming a pseudopod. When the endoplasm reaches the end of the foot, it turns into ectoplasm and flows backward inside the cell membrane. At the rear, ectoplasm turns into endoplasm and flows toward the foot (3).

cap

3

pseudopod

USING FEET TO FEED

Part of an amoeba's ectoplasm can be extended into a kind of limb called a pseudopod. This limb has two uses: it can pull the amoeba along, and it can be used for feeding. Amoebas usually feed on bacteria, simple algae, or other small single-celled organisms. They also play an important part in the decomposition of animal and plant matter in many aquatic habitats by feeding on small morsels of dead material.

When amoebas encounter a particle of food, they extend one or two pseudopods around the particle, literally engulfing it and swallowing it into their cell as they move toward it. Inside the cell the food is enclosed in a bubblelike cavity called a vacuole, where it is digested by enzymes released by the cell.

DANGEROUS PARASITES

When they are parasitic, amoebas can cause serious diseases, including dysentery and amebiasis in humans. These diseases produce symptoms such as diarrhea and dehydration in an affected person and can cause abscesses on several internal organs. They are spread by poor sanitation and can be picked up by drinking water contaminated with sewage or by eating unwashed fruits and vegetables. While these diseases can be treated with modern drugs, many sufferers are too poor to afford treatment, and thousands of people die each year from diseases caused by amoebas. ◆

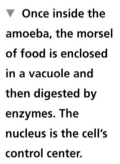

◄ An amoeba extends two pseudopods around a smaller protozoan before engulfing it.

pseudopod

SEE ALSO
• Algae
• Bacteria
• Fungi
• Plankton

▼ Once inside the amoeba, the morsel of food is enclosed in a vacuole and then digested by enzymes. The nucleus is the cell's control center.

nucleus

vacuoles containing partly digested prey

AMPHIBIAN

There are approximately 4,000 different species of amphibians found on Earth. Most inhabit warm, wet areas, ranging from swamps to moist forests. However, some amphibians exist in harsher climates, such as deserts and cool regions. Most amphibians spend at least one part of their life cycle in water. For example, many frogs start life as aquatic tadpoles before changing into adults that live on land. Amphibians lose water through their skin and must avoid drying out on land. There are three major groups of amphibians: frogs and toads, newts and salamanders, and caecilians.

PHYSICAL CHARACTERISTICS

Amphibians are vertebrates, which means that they have an internal skeleton with a backbone, similar to that found in birds and mammals. Most are relatively small: the North American

cricket frog grows to just over an inch (3 cm) long. However, hellbenders, the largest salamanders in North America, can reach 30 inches (76 cm) long. Most amphibians have moist, slimy skin. The slime is mucus secreted by the body to hold in moisture. It may also serve another function—protection. The mucus of many species is toxic to other animals. Predators that attempt to eat poisonous amphibians may gag, vomit, or even die. Many amphibians are brightly colored to warn predators of

▲ **This red-eyed tree frog has large feet with suction pads on its toes. These help it grip tightly to vertical surfaces, such as leaves and tree trunks. While the adults are mostly tree- or ground-dwelling, the young are free-swimming aquatic tadpoles.**

gills

◀ **Just before mating, the male Mexican axolotl instigates a courtship dance by nudging the female with his snout. The male then deposits his sperm on a rock, and the female picks it up with her cloaca (an opening at the rear). The sperm are stored inside in a saclike organ until fertilization. Axolotls are unusual salamanders that reach sexual maturity without changing form from the larval stage. They spend their whole life in water, keeping the external gills and broad tail typical of most larvae.**

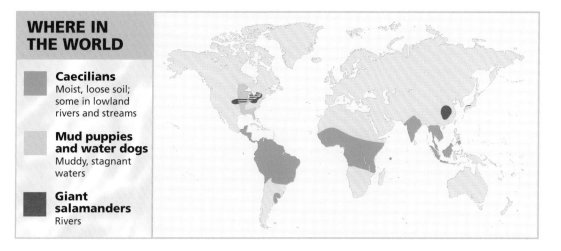

WHERE IN THE WORLD

Caecilians
Moist, loose soil; some in lowland rivers and streams

Mud puppies and water dogs
Muddy, stagnant waters

Giant salamanders
Rivers

▶ Chinese giant salamanders are even larger than North American hellbenders and can be as long as 6 feet (1.8 m). Giant salamanders are nocturnal and never leave their riverine homes, though they lose their larval gills.

their poisons so that they do not attempt to eat them in the first place. This is useful because, in general, amphibians are slow-moving creatures and cannot escape from their enemies easily. Frogs tend to be the quickest of the three groups of amphibians.

Frogs can be distinguished from other amphibians by their massive, elongated back legs, which they use for jumping and hopping. Salamanders resemble lizards somewhat, in that they have a slender body, a long tail, and four short legs. Caecilians are the most unusual looking of the amphibians; these legless creatures look like large earthworms. The long, slender body of caecilians is covered with ringlike grooves that help the animals when burrowing.

SENSES AND FEEDING
Salamanders and caecilians do not have a well-developed sense of hearing like mammals do, and they cannot hear airborne sounds well. However, they are able to feel sounds traveling through the ground or water as vibrations. These vibrations are picked up by the animals' skeleton and are transmitted to the bones of the inner ear. The ears of frogs and toads include a layer of skin on the

outside of the body that transmits vibrations in the air to the bones inside the ear; this allows them to hear airborne sounds much better than other groups of amphibians do.

Salamanders and caecilians have poor eyesight—some of them are even blind. Frogs and toads, however, have relatively good vision. Their eyes are particularly well adapted for detecting moving objects, and many species will attack anything that moves and is a suitable size to eat: if the item is not edible, they spit it out. Salamanders and caecilians have a very well-developed sense of smell, and caecilians can also detect vibrations in the ground. Frogs have a poor sense of smell and so rely on their eyesight. All amphibians are predators, eating insects and soft-bodied invertebrates such as worms and spiders. Some will also eat smaller amphibians, fish, reptiles, birds, and mammals.

▲ A common newt swims underwater. Newts are carnivorous animals that prey on insects, worms, slugs, and small fish. They have flattened tails that help with swimming.

Salamanders and caecilians are fossorial animals, which means they dig underground or under vegetation and debris. These animals are mostly sit-and-wait predators: they wait for prey to come to them rather than actively seeking out food. Some frogs and salamanders have a long sticky tongue that shoots out to capture prey. Caecilians grab their prey with their mouth. All amphibians swallow food whole because they are unable to chew.

COLD-BLOODED

Amphibians are often described as cold-blooded. This term is misleading, though, as cold-blooded animals are not necessarily cold. Instead, their body temperature is determined by the temperature of their environment, and they are unable to produce their own body heat as mammals and birds do. To warm up, amphibians move to a warm area, such as a patch of sunlight; and to cool down they retreat underground, underwater, or into the shade.

The major advantage of being cold-blooded is that amphibians require less food to survive than do warm-blooded

▲ This illustration shows two caecilians searching for prey on a riverbed. The favorite food items of these limbless amphibians are invertebrates such as earthworms and termites.

FACT FILE

Caecilians
Limbless amphibians of the order Gymnophiona; found in loose, moist soil and rivers in tropical areas worldwide; they are worm-like and adapted to burrowing; all caecilians have poor eyesight; some are blind, with eyes covered by bone or skin; they hunt by smell and by sensing vibrations in the ground

animals of a similar size. This is because cold-blooded animals do not burn energy from their food to keep their body warm. By contrast, a mammal needs to consume large amounts of food, since it must constantly burn energy to maintain its body temperature. Mammals require as much as 95 percent more energy to survive than amphibians do.

The disadvantage of being cold-blooded is that an amphibian's life is controlled by the weather. Unlike warm-blooded animals, amphibians cannot be active when it is very cold. Many amphibians hibernate in extreme cold weather and wait until it warms up enough to move around. Remarkably, some species of frogs and salamanders have been observed moving in water under ice, especially during the spring.

BREATHING AND REPRODUCTION

The skin of amphibians is permeable, so it allows water, oxygen, and other substances to move through it. As a result, amphibians can breathe through their skin. Some salamanders do not have lungs and rely entirely on this method of breathing.

Frogs and toads are the only amphibians that use sounds to communicate with each other. (The salamanders called mud puppies and water dogs were named when people thought they produced sounds like dogs. This is now known not to be the case.) During the breeding season, male frogs inflate their throat with air and create loud whistles and croaks to attract the females. Females then choose a male to mate with. While mating, the female releases hundreds of eggs and the male releases sperm, which fertilize the eggs. After

hatching, the tadpoles stay in the water until they change (metamorphose) into little froglets. Most tadpoles are free-swimming animals that hunt prey. In a few species the young forms are immobile, feeding on the yolk from their egg until they develop into froglets.

The reproduction of salamanders and newts varies greatly, but most have elaborate courtship rituals. Depending on altitude, Alpine black salamanders, which bear live young, can have the longest gestation period on Earth: 38 months. All caecilians undergo internal fertilization, with some laying fertilized eggs and others bearing live young. ◆

SEE ALSO
• Frog
• Lake and pond
• Newt
• Salamander

▼ These common frog tadpoles have just hatched and will metamorphose into adults within two to three months. Tadpoles have tails for swimming, but adult frogs do not.

ANGELFISH

Angelfish are among the most colorful and graceful of all fish. The emperor angelfish is probably one of the best-known species because it is a popular aquarium fish.

Angelfish belong to the family Pomacanthidae (poe-muh-KANTH-ih-dee), which contains more than 70 species, mostly found in the western Pacific and Indian Oceans. Only nine species occur in the Atlantic and four in the eastern Pacific. All angelfish in this family are marine; generally living near coral reefs at depths of less than 7 feet (2 m). One exception is the black-banded angelfish, which is usually found 80–90 feet (24–27 m) below the surface in the waters around Hawaii.

Most angelfish species are omnivorous, feeding on a wide variety of small animals, including corals. Some species have a more specialized diet, however: for example, the lemon peel angelfish prefers to eat algae; the black-banded angelfish feeds on sponges; and a species called the old woman feeds on microscopic plankton.

HIGHLIGHTING THE DIFFERENCES

The body of the angelfish is oval and flattened from side to side. Adults are usually small, measuring around 4 inches (10 cm) long, and only a few species, such as the old woman, can reach a length of 20 inches (50 cm). Young angelfish have very different color patterns compared to adults, and

▲ The coral reef-dwelling French angelfish grows up to 15 inches (38 cm) long. It has bright yellow highlights on its dark scales. Divers have noticed that if they swim above one of these fish it will turn on its side to keep a better eye on them. Young French angelfish often clean parasites off larger fish.

WHERE IN THE WORLD

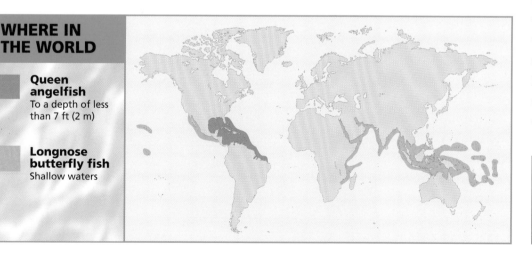

Queen angelfish
To a depth of less than 7 ft (2 m)

Longnose butterfly fish
Shallow waters

SEE ALSO

• Coral reef
• Fish
• Locomotion

some undergo extraordinary changes in their appearance as they grow.

Angelfish are very similar to butterfly fish, but angelfish have a strong spine on the lower rear corner of the preopercle—a flat plate that overlaps the gill cover below the eye. There is a group of freshwater angelfish that is also popular with people who keep aquariums. However, these fish belong to the family Cichlidae (SIK-luh-dee) and are not related to marine angelfish.

BUTTERFLY FISH

Butterfly fish are closely related to angelfish, and until the mid-1970s they were classified in the same family: the Chaetodontidae (keed-oe-DAHN-tuh-dee). There are more than 100 species of butterfly fish, found on coral reefs in tropical seas. Like angelfish, butterfly fish have brightly colored patterns on their bodies, including black spots on the sides of some species. These spots resemble eyes and are very effective in

◄ The longnose butterfly fish has very long jaws. It uses these to pick out small invertebrates sheltering among the spines of sea urchins and in the crevices of coral reefs.

confusing predators so that they cannot tell the head from the tail.

The larval (immature) stage in butterfly fish lasts for two or three months; the larvae float in the plankton. Larvae from different species often look very different from each other because they have several head bones modified into thin plates that can expand in different ways.

Adults from different species also have a wide variety of jaw shapes, which reflect their different feeding habits. For example, the Indo-Pacific maypole butterfly fish has short jaws and feeds on tiny animals called polyps that make up coral colonies. Other species have long jaws to feed in crevices in coral. Most butterfly fish live a solitary life or wander through the reef in small groups of two or three. ◆

FACT FILE

Name
Queen angelfish (*Holacanthus ciliaris*)

Distinctive features
Yellow tail and pectoral fins; spot on nape is ringed and dotted with bright blue; young have four narrow, curved, light blue bars on dark background

Habitat
Coral reefs

Behavior
Solitary, or in very small groups

Food
Coral polyps, small invertebrates, algae

Breeding
Throughout year

Size
Generally 10 in (25 cm) long, but can be up to 1 ft (30 cm)

◄ As they develop from juveniles (far left) to adults (left), emperor angelfish change dramatically in color. The young of this reef-dwelling species are dark, with a pattern of concentric pale lines. The adults are patterned with many diagonal lines.

ANGLERFISH

FACT FILE

Name
Monkfish
(*Lophius
piscatorius*)

**Distinctive
features**
Broad mouth and
head; small eyes
on top of head

Habitat
Sandy, gravelly, or
muddy seafloors

Food
Smaller fish

Breeding
Spawn in late
winter, spring,
and summer;
eggs are laid in
large sheets

Lifespan
Not known

Size
Up to 7 ft
(2 m) long

There are nearly 300 species of anglerfish, grouped in several families. These include species of goosefish, frogfish, and batfish. The feature all anglerfish have in common, and for which they are named, is a long, bony rod with a little piece of flesh dangling from the end. This structure—which looks like a fishing rod with bait—is actually a part of the front dorsal fin that has moved forward gradually as the fish has evolved. When any form of food, such as a fish or a large invertebrate, comes close to the bait, the anglerfish opens its enormous mouth in a rapid reflex movement and sucks its victim in. This reflex is one of the quickest movements in the animal world. The length of the fishing rod, or lure, varies between species, from less than half of the diameter of the bait to three times the length of the fish.

▲ **Monkfish move very little from their position on the seabed. They attract small fish by twitching the fleshy lobe at the end of the first dorsal ray. They also prey on practically any bottom-living organism.**

GOOSEFISH

Goosefish, such as the monkfish, lie in wait for their prey and are almost invisible as they lurk on the seabed. This is because the color of their skin is a good match for the sand or gravel of their surroundings. Goosefish live in the sea at a wide range of depths, from inshore to up to 1,800 feet (550 m) deep. Some goosefish reach 7 feet (2 m) in length.

▲ **Many frogfish are well camouflaged on the seabed. This one looks like a sponge.**

FROGFISH

Frogfish and batfish are found only in tropical and subtropical seas. Frogfish are usually small, some measuring less than 4 inches (10 cm) long, with only a few species reaching 16 inches (41 cm). They live in clear, shallow water on reefs and rocky bottoms, with the exception of the marbled frogfish, which swims in the open ocean. The marbled frogfish has grasping pectoral fins, which it can use for moving on floating seaweed. There is also an Indo-Australian species, *Antennarius biocellatus*, that is the only frogfish to live in brackish and freshwaters.

BATFISH

Batfish have a very broad and flattened head and trunk, circular or triangular in shape and covered by strong scales. They usually grow to around 8 inches (20 cm) long, but the shortnosed, or red-bellied, batfish can reach 16 inches (41 cm). Batfish are very awkward swimmers and have adapted to walk on the seabed, using their large armlike pectoral fins and smaller pelvic fins. The lure is very short in these species, and the bait may produce substances to attract the prey.

◄ **Female deep-sea angler-fish have luminous lures that attract prey in the pitch-black waters.**

DEEP-SEA ANGLERFISH

Some species of anglerfish are typical inhabitants of deep waters, between 3,300 feet (1,000 m) and 12,000 feet (3,700 m). These fish are usually small: most measure less than 3 inches (8 cm). However, one species, *Ceratias holboelli*, reaches at least 47 inches (1.2 m) long. Deep-sea angler-fish live in the dark waters on the bottom of the oceans, and their lure and bait are luminescent: they contain light-producing bacteria. ◆

▲ **Male deep-sea anglerfish are much smaller than the females, reaching only 5 to 10 percent of the length of their mates. A male locates a female by smell, then attaches himself to her and lives as a parasite. After breeding, he does not detach but grows into her body.**

WHERE IN THE WORLD

Monkfish
Seabed from 60 to 1,800 ft (18 to 550 m) deep

American goosefish
Seabed from 60 to 1,800 ft (18 to 550 m) deep

SEE ALSO

• Bioluminescence
• Deep-sea organism
• Ocean floor

ANTARCTIC OCEAN

◄ Near the southern tip of South America, Le Maire Channel separates the islands of Tierra del Fuego and Isla de los Estados. During the winter months ice makes the passage between the South Atlantic and the South Pacific hazardous for ships.

SEE ALSO
- Atlantic Ocean
- Global warming
- Iceberg
- Indian Ocean
- Pacific Ocean
- Penguin

Around the continent of Antarctica the ocean forms an open band around Earth. Here, only the very southern tips of South America, Africa, and Australia intrude. This is the Antarctic, or Southern, Ocean. This huge expanse of water connects most of the oceans into one great body of water—a global ocean. Since there is little land to define its limits (only 20 percent of land is in the Southern Hemisphere), the borders of the Antarctic Ocean are not easily defined. In fact, it is not properly an ocean in its own right but the combined southern parts of the Atlantic, Indian, and Pacific Oceans. However, the Antarctic Ocean is usually considered to extend from the edge of Antarctica to 60 degrees south.

THE WORLD'S COLDEST PLACE
Unlike the Arctic Ocean, which is the ocean that sits on top of the world, the Antarctic Ocean forms a ring of water around a frozen continent. The cold landmass surrounding the South Pole chills the waters of the Antarctic to temperatures even below freezing—the salt content of the seawater prevents it from freezing at 32°F (0°C). Yet most of the Antarctic Ocean does not freeze solid like the landlocked Arctic does. Only places like the Weddell Sea, which is somewhat enclosed by the curve of the Antarctic Peninsula, contain solid ice all year around. Even so, waters

▼ An Antarctic bald cod feeds on algae on the underside of the ice. Antarctic cod are the most common fish in the Antarctic Ocean. These fish are related to icefish, and the different species have a variety of lifestyles. Antarctic cod range in size from 4 inches (10 cm) to more than 6 feet (1.8 m) long.

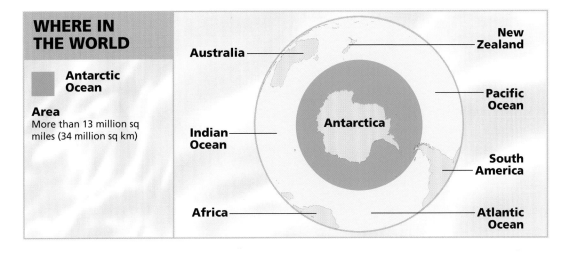

WHERE IN THE WORLD

Antarctic Ocean

Area
More than 13 million sq miles (34 million sq km)

Australia

New Zealand

Pacific Ocean

Antarctica

Indian Ocean

South America

Africa

Atlantic Ocean

from the Antarctic travel northward and help keep Earth cool.

The continent of Antarctica holds 90 percent of all the ice on the planet. Great ice sheets cover the land, and the ice shelves that extend into the ocean are 300 to 600 feet (90 to 180 m) thick. Icebergs in the Antarctic Ocean are usually flat-topped sheets formed when the ice shelves break up, rather than the pointy chunks of broken glaciers found in the Arctic Ocean. An iceberg was recently sighted that was bigger than the state of Delaware. Some scientists are concerned that the breakup of the ice shelves in the Antarctic may be a sign that Earth's climate is warming up too much (global warming).

RICH WATERS AND ANTIFREEZE FISH

Where the cold waters of the Antarctic meet warmer water, upwelling occurs. An upwelling is a vertical current that brings rich nutrients to the surface of the ocean. There, sunlight encourages the growth of great accumulations, or blooms, of plankton. In these waters krill—small shrimplike creatures 2 inches (5 cm) long—form a key element in the food webs that support the abundant life of the Antarctic Ocean.

Penguins, squid, fish, and the world's largest whales feed on the krill. People once hunted whales throughout the Antarctic Ocean.

In the deep waters of the Antarctic Ocean there are fish that have evolved to live in water at temperatures that would freeze the blood of other species. Unlike the blood of other fish, icefish blood contains an antifreeze chemical. As a result these fish live comfortably in the world's coldest waters. ◆

▼ **Several species of penguins inhabit the Antarctic Ocean. These flightless birds have few predators and feed mainly on fish.**

AQUACULTURE

The growing or raising of aquatic plants and animals by people is called aquaculture. An alternative name is underwater farming. Aquaculture has a 2,500-year history, but it may be up to 4,000 years since the first freshwater carp were raised in China. Today, both freshwater and marine species are farmed by aquaculturists.

PURPOSES

There are many reasons for culturing aquatic species. An important one is to produce food for people. Shrimp, clams, oysters, salmon, trout, catfish, and many other species are grown by fish farmers in order to supply the high demand for seafood. Some aquaculturists raise fish for stocking recreational and commercial fisheries. The fish are usually raised through the early stages of development, when losses would be greatest in

the wild, then released into a suitable habitat where they can reach maturity. Other fish farmers raise ornamental species for use in home aquariums and backyard ponds.

CULTURE SYSTEMS

Most aquaculture facilities use ponds. Aquaculture ponds need a reliable source of water and should be equipped with drains so that the water can be removed quickly and easily when necessary. Usually, once a pond is filled, no additional water is added except to replace the amount that evaporates (becomes water vapor). Raceways are usually rectangular or round concrete, fiberglass, or metal containers through which water flows continuously. In flow-through systems, the water is discarded at the same rate that it enters; in closed systems the water is recirculated. In a closed system the discarded water is treated to remove harmful

▲ **Kuruma prawns in a Taiwanese aquaculture facility's observation tank, where their health and development can be checked. Crustaceans make up only about one percent of worldwide aquaculture production, whereas fish and mollusks account for about a third each. Seaweed accounts for around one quarter.**

SEE ALSO

▲ **Carp were probably the first fish to be raised artificially. Here, they are shown being harvested at a fish farm in Israel.**

waste substances, then returned to the raceway. Such systems can be used when water supplies are limited or expensive. Net pens are used in the ocean for raising salmon and other fish. They are large, floating cages usually located in sheltered bays. More than 40,000 fish can be reared in one 20,000-square-foot (1,860-sq-m) pen. Net pens that can be used in rougher offshore waters are being developed as space and high-quality water is becoming increasingly scarce in coastal areas.

FARM MANAGEMENT

Aquaculturists must frequently check water temperature, dissolved oxygen, and several other factors so that they can take corrective action if a problem that threatens the health of the cultured organisms is discovered. They must, in most cases, provide feed for the animals. They must also check for diseases and treat sick animals. Aquaculturists may also need to breed the species they are raising. Unless a farmer is only interested in raising young animals to maturity, the farmer will need to have

considerable knowledge on breeding, spawning, hatching, and rearing the animals. Hence, many of those involved in aquaculture are biologists.

CONCERNS

Aquaculture can relieve pressure on wild stocks, but it can be an intensive farming practice; some people are concerned that fish, in particular, suffer from being farmed this way. Pens can be cramped and overcrowded, so the fish have no room to move around. Many become infected with fish lice, parasites that feed on the fish's tissues. Excessively high levels of fish lice infestations spread by fish farms have been blamed for the falling levels of wild salmon populations in Scotland. ◆

◀ The raceways of a private rainbow trout farm. The water used by such freshwater fish farms has to be carefully managed. Nearby rivers or coasts can be polluted if large amounts of fish feces are released into the environment, causing algal blooms that kill wildlife.

FACT FILE

Aquaculture
The farming of aquatic organisms, including fish, algae, and shellfish, in either salt water or freshwater

Mariculture
Aquaculture carried out in the sea

Production
About 100 million tons of aquatic species are marketed in the world each year; about 20 percent of the total is from aquaculture, and this proportion is increasing

Top crop
More carp are raised than any other species or species group; the vast majority of carp produced are raised and eaten in China

▶ A Scottish sea pen for farming salmon. The pen can be raised or lowered and includes floating spars and a circular rim, features that help it move with the currents, tides, and waves instead of opposing them. Sea pens allow the sea to refresh the farmed animals' water supply and remove their wastes naturally.

AQUARIUM

Whether it's a class trip to a public aquarium or a goldfish in a home tank, many young people in the United States experience aquatic life for the first time in an aquarium. Aquariums are places to keep fish and other aquatic life. The Latin words *aqua*, which means "water," and *arium*, which means "a place for," are combined to give a name for both 10-gallon (38-liter) home tanks for pet guppies and for the modern, multimillion-gallon enclosures that house killer whales or even whale sharks 30 feet (9 m) long.

The beginning of aquariums as they are known today was in Victorian England in the 19th century. A popular hobby of the time was to display ferns and other plants in glass cases called terrariums (from the Latin words *terra*, which means "earth," and *arium*); it soon became common for these to be used to contain water and fish, too. These clear-sided, simple containers have become bigger and bigger over the years. Silicone glue now bonds glass panels together, eliminating the need for metal framing, and the glass is often replaced by acrylic (plastic) panels that can be molded into curves and even bubbles, making the aquarium as much a piece of architecture as a container.

THE FISH HOBBY INDUSTRY

Goldfish are hardy enough to be kept in simple glass bowls, but most fish require pumps and filters to provide the animals with a suitable environment. All this equipment is readily available through pet stores and aquarium shops. It may be surprising to some, but fish hobbyists support an industry that is

▲ A sheet of acrylic separates visitors from jellyfish at the Monterey Bay Aquarium, California.

▶ Some popular home aquarium species. The sword-tail is a relative of the common gold-fish. Male guppies are more colorful than females, but it is not always easy to sex fish: both male and female neon tetras are colorful. Invertebrates such as snails can also be kept in aquariums.

second only to that of photographers in the amount of money spent on their interest each year.

COLLECTORS AND FISH FARMERS

Fish are still collected all over the world to supply aquariums. South American and Indonesian rivers, for example, are fished for rare specimens. Many people are concerned about the impact of this on wild populations. However, a great number of fish are now raised on fish farms, many of which are located in Florida and throughout Asia. For shipping, the fish are placed in plastic bags of water, inflated with oxygen and sealed within Styrofoam boxes to protect them from extreme temperatures. This method, combined with modern air transport, means the fish can be shipped to almost any point on the globe within 48 hours. Many freshwater fish hobbyists have perfected their methods enough to breed fish such as angelfish and discus. Often they supply pet stores or other hobbyists with their surplus fish. Some commercial fish farmers were hobbyists that saw their tanks expand from a single tank in the living room, to 10 in the basement, to hundreds in the garage, and then to a full-scale fish farm.

ANGELFISH

One of the most popular fish in the home aquarium is the striking angelfish. The stately elegance of this fish has captured the fascination of many freshwater hobbyists. In nature it is found in thickly planted parts of the Amazon, and its silvery body and dark stripes help it to blend in with its surroundings. In the aquarium, however, it stands out as a regal showpiece. Angelfish live

FACT FILE

Home aquarium
All aquariums need to provide the right conditions to support aquatic life. The species and genders of animals need to be selected carefully to avoid loss by predation or fighting

Equipment
Tank, with cover to retain heat and keep fish inside; filters and filtration system to keep the water clean; air pump to supply oxygen; heater and thermometer to control temperature

Food
Most home aquarium fish are fed once a day on live or processed brine shrimp, water fleas (*Daphnia*), and red worms (*Tubifex*)

black lace angelfish

male guppy

female guppy

swordtail

aquatic plants

neon tetras

ram

nail

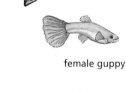
clown loach

peacefully, their care is relatively undemanding, and they breed with just one mate.

Male and female angelfish look very much alike; only experts can tell them apart. Most angelfish are raised in captivity, and a number of hybrids show special coloration and other features. For example, extra-long fins are prominent on the veiltail angelfish.

SALTWATER AQUARIUMS

In recent years, equipment has been developed that supports the keeping of saltwater fish and invertebrates, such as shrimp, corals, and sea anemones, in home aquariums. For example, salt formulas have been developed that simply require pouring in the formula and adding water.

Advancements such as these have allowed even the brilliant fish of the coral reefs to be kept at home. The requirements for saltwater aquariums are more demanding than those for freshwater aquariums, but hobbyists are learning more and more about marine fish and their behavior.

▼ Unusual aquatic species, such as this brightly colored sea slug, are often kept under strictly controlled conditions in laboratory aquariums so that scientists can make detailed studies of how they live, feed, and reproduce.

PUBLIC AQUARIUMS

The world's first public aquarium was opened in 1854 at the London Zoological Society (London Zoo). Biologist Philip Gosse persuaded the zoological garden to allow him space to display aquatic animals in glass cases. The

▼ Many public aquariums have open touch pools that contain aquatic animals commonly found in rock pools on the seashore. This girl is reaching over to touch a starfish in a pool at the Sentosa Island Aquarium in Singapore.

SEE ALSO

• Amazon River
• Angelfish
• Aquaculture
• Carp family
• Cichlid
• Conservation
• Fishing
• Mantis shrimp
• Nature preserve

exhibit was so popular that other public aquariums were soon built in Berlin, Naples, and Paris.

In 1969 a second "golden age" began when the City of Boston helped the New England Aquarium open on what had been a broken-down waterfront. Combined with new shops in a restored marketplace, the aquarium became an attraction for Boston citizens, schoolchildren, and tourists. This formula of waterfront, public aquarium, and marketplace was successfully repeated in Baltimore, Maryland, and, later, in a number of other U.S. cities.

There were problems at first, since some marine animals proved difficult to keep. It was discovered that seals can live in freshwater without any major problems. When dolphins were first kept, also in freshwater, they developed skin conditions that could be fatal. It is now known that dolphins are more sensitive to water conditions, including salinity, than was previously thought.

Public aquariums are able to display animals in huge tanks in settings that mimic their natural surroundings. They give visitors a view of underwater life otherwise available only to scuba divers. However, some people are concerned that public aquariums take animals from the wild and keep them captive in unnatural settings. Public aquariums believe that the care they give their animals is as good, if not better, than the hard life the animals would face in the wild. Proof of this is that nowadays even marine mammals live a long life and often breed in aquarium tanks. Almost all the dolphins, seals, and sea lions seen in public aquariums have been born there as part of captive-breeding programs.

Public aquariums are also part of the network of institutions that rescue and rehabilitate stranded animals that have been washed up along the coastline. People who manage public aquariums also believe that the value and inspiration given to the many visitors helps the conservation of wild populations: the general public will better protect, and is more likely to pressure policy makers to protect, an environment that they understand. Most public aquariums have active education departments that work with schoolteachers to bring these messages to children. ◆

▲ **There are more than 2,000 marine mammals in sea parks around the United States. Popular campaigns often call for the release of larger animals, such as this killer whale, back into the wild. Releasing captive animals is problematic, though, and not always successful.**

AQUATIC PLANT

Plants live in a wide range of watery habitats, wherever they are exposed to the light that they need to photosynthesize. Photosynthesis is the process by which these organisms convert inorganic compounds to the sugars they need to survive. The energy for this process is obtained from sunlight. So, plants can live only where there is a good deal of light, and they are not found in deep-sea environments, where the light diminishes rapidly with depth.

Aquatic plants live almost entirely in freshwater, and few flowering plants live in the sea. The best-known example is eelgrass, or seagrass, which is probably a terrestrial plant that has returned to the sea. This plant grows in warm shallow water, where it forms large clumps of slim, tapelike leaves up to 6 feet (1.8 m) long. It is pollinated under water. Seaweeds are algae that look a bit like and photosynthesize like higher plants but have different lifestyles.

ADAPTING TO SUBMERGED LIFE

Some completely aquatic plants are able to overcome the problems of a life in

▲ **Spring-tape (or strapleaf) forms tall, underwater meadows in fast-flowing springs and streams. The ribbon-like leaves are about ¾ inch (2 cm) wide and between 2 and 3 ft (60 to 90 cm) long. Their straplike shape allows them to bend and flex with the water currents.**

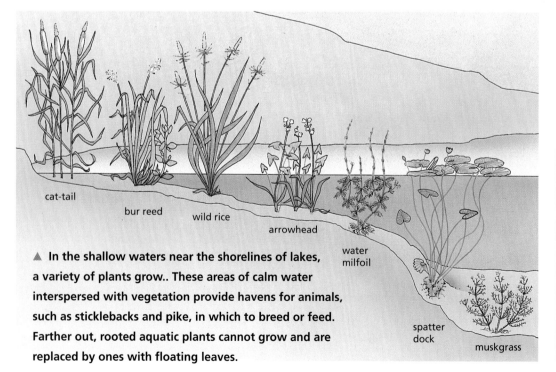

cat-tail
bur reed
wild rice
arrowhead
water milfoil
spatter dock
muskgrass

▲ **In the shallow waters near the shorelines of lakes, a variety of plants grow.. These areas of calm water interspersed with vegetation provide havens for animals, such as sticklebacks and pike, in which to breed or feed. Farther out, rooted aquatic plants cannot grow and are replaced by ones with floating leaves.**

SEE ALSO

- Bladderwort
- Eelgrass
- Everglades
- Duckweed
- Mangrove
- Photosynthesis
- Pondweed
- Reproduction
- Water hyacinth
- Water lily

▲ Also known as the anglepod blue flag, the prairie iris grows abundantly in swamps, on cypress prairies, and along marshy shores.

deep water, where there is a lack of light for photosynthesis. For example, water lilies do this by sending up their leaves on long stalks, which float on the surface in the sunlight. Other modifications are common in submerged plants. For example, in order to get oxygen down to the roots, some water plants have developed a system of hollow stems that allows oxygen to pass down and waste carbon dioxide gas to pass up

and leave the plant from the leaf surface. This has the advantage of allowing the plant's roots to grow healthily while buried in mud containing almost no oxygen. Without this mechanism they would rot and die.

Terrestrial plants depend on the evaporation of water from the surface of their leaves to draw up nourishment from their roots. This evaporation cannot take place from submerged leaves, however, so nutrients are transported by roots that build up pressure and pump the nutrient-containing liquid up the stems. For this reason, ordinary terrestrial plants cannot survive long if they are submerged for long periods.

EXPLOITING AQUATIC HABITATS

Aquatic plants growing in freshwater are exposed to a wide range of environmental conditions, and their shape and habit is modified to make the most of their surroundings. Many plants growing submerged in ponds and lakes, for example, form large clumps with finely divided fernlike leaves to increase

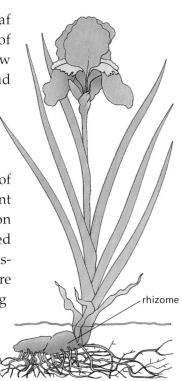

rhizome

▲ Plants that grow in wetlands, such as this iris, often have underground stems called rhizomes. These link individual above ground stems, making the plants more stable.

◄ The Ogeechee lime inhabits the edges of riverbanks or the margins of lakes, where its branches overhang the water. When its fruit becomes ripe it falls into the water and is eaten by aquatic animals that disperse the seeds and allow new plants to grow.

their surface area as much as possible. This in turn increases the rate at which they can absorb nutrients from the water and carry out photosynthesis, so these plants grow very rapidly. These types of water plant are an important food source for waterfowl.

If there was a strong current, however, the fragile ferny leaves of these aquatic plants would be swept together and damaged. Plants growing submerged in currents usually have slim, straplike leaves that do not resist the water flow, or are low-growing and mossy so that they are not damaged by the currents.

Some plants have the best of both worlds, with underwater foliage typical of aquatic plants and floating leaves on the surface. Most aquatic plants found in freshwater send their flower stems above the surface, so the flowers can be pollinated by insects.

Many aquatic plants float completely on the surface of lakes and rivers, and their roots absorb nutrients from the water. Duckweed is a common example of this type of plant. Another example is the water hyacinth, which floats on gas-filled bladders and grows very rapidly in tropical regions. This plant illustrates

the danger of introducing plants into new habitats, because introduced water hyacinths now clog up waterways all over the world.

Although eelgrass is truly aquatic, there are some other plants growing in or near the sea that are semi-aquatic.

▲ The water-spider orchid, pictured here, can be seen in wet meadows or in mats of vegetation floating on lakes.

◄ The flower (far left) and fruit (left) of the American, or yellow, lotus. This plant is a relative of the water lily and inhabits ponds, marshes, and sluggish streams. The seeds can be seen inside individual sections of the fruit.

▶ Pitcher plants are tall carnivorous plants that thrive in moist, humid forests and bogs.

▼ Each pitcher plant has large, trumpet-shaped leaves with a lid, called an operculum. The leaves are often brightly colored and covered in nectar to attract insects, which fall in to the digestive juices at the base of the pitcher and are prevented from escaping by long, downward-pointing hairs.

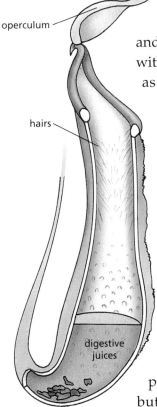

operculum

hairs

digestive juices

lengthwise section of leaf

Mangrove trees, for example, have roots that are submerged at high tide. Because there is no oxygen in the mud in which they grow, their roots emerge and point upward so that they can absorb oxygen from the air and from water flowing around them at high tide.

Salt marshes are another type of extreme habitat with which some aquatic plants have to cope. The sea covers plants that grow in salt marshes only occasionally, but they still need mechanisms to protect them from damage caused by salt. They absorb the salt through the roots but then excrete it through their leaves.

Another extreme environment is the bog habitat, where the brown water is very rich in organic materials that have dissolved from rotting vegetation. However, this water is very low in essential minerals—especially nitrogen. Some bog plants have developed a carnivorous lifestyle, and their insect prey provides them with the nitrogen they need. Some, such as bladderworts, are completely submerged, while others grow above the water surface or in very wet soil near the water's edge. The familiar Venus's-flytrap and trumpetlike pitcher plants are typical bog plants of this type.

USEFUL PLANTS

Many partly submerged plants can grow for a while under water but eventually die unless they are exposed to the air from time to time. Rice is a good example of a cultivated plant that must grow partly submerged for most of its life but ripens only when the water is drained from the flooded fields.

Reeds grow with their roots submerged and line the banks of most rivers. They are widely used as roofing material throughout developing countries, and recently they have been used in water purification factories. There, water polluted with sewage is run over their roots, and most of the waste substances it contains are absorbed and can be removed from the system when the reeds are cut down. Floating plants such as water hyacinth and duckweed have been used for the same purpose.

Papyrus is a very large aquatic reed that is found in the Tropics and grows nearly 10 feet (3 m) high over several years. It was once a source of writing material for the Egyptians, who dried and flattened the stems to make a material very similar to paper. ◆

ARAPAIMA

Once a staple food of the people living along the Amazon River, the giant arapaima is a fish that is difficult to find today. It has been reported to reach a length of 15 feet (4.5 m), but the individuals observed recently average about 8 feet (2.4 m) in length. Some beluga sturgeon and tropical catfish can grow larger than this, but the arapaima is certainly one of the world's largest freshwater fish. The arapaima is found in the rivers and lakes of the Amazon drainage basin in Peru and Brazil. It is known by the names *paiche* in Peru and *pirarucu* in Brazil.

The arapaima is a member of a family of fish with the common name of bonytongues. The tongues of these fish are indeed bony—so bony that people use the tongue as a food grater and scraper. Bonytongues are found in African, Asian, South American, and Indo-Australian freshwaters. The fact that these related species live so far apart today is evidence that the continents were probably once joined together far back in time.

AIR BREATHER

The arapaima is unable to survive only on the oxygen its gills extract from the water. Its swim bladder is richly supplied with blood vessels and is connected to the throat. It can be used as a lung, since it can absorb oxygen from air. (The swim bladder in most other fish is generally closed and serves only as a flotation device.) The ability of the

▲ The arapaima is a formidable hunter. Smaller fish make up most of its diet, but the arapaima has also been known to leap from the water to snatch birds from overhanging trees.

WHERE IN THE WORLD

Arapaima
Rivers and lakes

Amazon

SEE ALSO

• Amazon River
• Fish
• River and stream

arapaima to take in gulps of air is important when the dry season reduces the river to murky, stagnant pools. Because the fish breathes air, however, it has to come to the surface of the water every 10 to 20 minutes, making it a target for people fishing with harpoons.

Harpooning a large arapaima is no easy feat. To bring one in is a test of strength in many cultures. The thick, bony scales of the arapaima are worn with pride on headbands and necklaces by native South Americans.

NEST BUILDERS

During the breeding season arapaima move into shallow, sandy areas to build their nests, fanning their fins to hollow out nests in the sand. Each nest is about 20 inches (50 cm) across and 6 inches (15 cm) deep. There the adults will protect the young fish until they reach a length of over 6 inches (15 cm), so giving their offspring a head start into the world. The same nest may be used over and over again.

A MAGNIFICENT FISH IN DECLINE

The numbers and size of the arapaima have declined throughout its range. The most serious depletion has been in a radius of a day's trip from human population centers. Fishers can go that far and bring the fish to market without refrigeration. This has spared some of the more remote areas from overfishing. The meat is highly prized and is cut into strips to dry. If refrigeration becomes available in areas away from the cities, greater exploitation is likely. ◆

FACT FILE

Name
Arapaima, paiche, or pirarucu
(*Arapaima gigas*)

Distinctive features
Very large; thick, horny scales

Habitat
Rivers and lakes in South America

Behavior
Comes to surface to breathe air, supplementing gill intake; has been known to leap from water

Food
Smaller fish, birds

Breeding
Lays around 47,000 eggs in nest among submerged plants

Size
Up to 15 ft (4.5 m) long; weighs up to 440 lb (200 kg)

◀ The arapaima builds a nest in submerged vegetation that will be guarded by both parents. Once they are swimming, the young fish (fry) will cluster around one parent's head. The fry are thought to feed on mucus secreted by the parent's skin.

ARCHAEOLOGY

The violent waters of the sea have swallowed many towns and cities of ancient civilizations and pioneering sailing expeditions and battleships. Underwater archaeologists study submerged ruins and wrecks to reveal their secrets for modern historians. While archaeologists have been excavating digs on land for many decades, the sea has safely held its treasures until only relatively recently.

The first underwater archaeological explorations were made in the 1850s, when the waters of a Swiss lake retreated during a drought and exposed pots, ornaments, weapons, and other remains of a prehistoric village. With the invention of subaqueous equipment and sophisticated exploration technology, archaeologists have moved their work to the deeper waters of the ocean. In 1960 George Bass directed the first

underwater excavation of a ship from the Bronze Age (4000 to 1000 B.C.E.), which was wrecked off Cape Gelidonya in Turkey in 1300 B.C.E. His work laid the foundations for other pioneering investigations, including the raising of the hull remains of the *Mary Rose*, a

▲ Divers prepare to explore the wreck of the *Lusitania*, a U.S. liner sunk in 1915 by a German U-boat in the Irish Sea. Early divers had to wear heavy suits to make them sink, and some were limited by the amount of air they could take down with them.

◄ A scuba diver in a lightweight wetsuit, carrying enough air for an hour or two, inspects a site.

SEE ALSO
• Exploration
• Scuba diving and snorkeling

Tudor battleship that sank off the coast of southern England 400 years ago.

UNDERWATER EXCAVATIONS

Finding wrecks and ruins underwater is a great challenge. Often simple methods, such as asking local sponge divers for information, can produce exciting results. However, three main technological instruments are available: sonar can show up the shape of the seabed; a sonic profiler can detect buried objects; and magnetic scanners can detect changes in Earth's magnetic field caused by large metal objects.

Once sites are located precisely, archaeologists can carry out detailed excavations. Grids are laid out so that the position and depth of finds can be accurately mapped. In order to minimize clouding of the water by sediment, airlifts are used to suck up silt from the area. Smaller objects can be retrieved by hand, but heavier finds are lifted using air-filled balloons known as lift bags, which float upward, carrying even the heaviest loads. Great care must be taken to preserve underwater finds. If they are exposed to the air or are allowed to dry out they can rapidly rust or crumble.

Early underwater investigators were sometimes motivated by the prospect of finding lost treasure chests. In the past, many treasures were lost to private collectors, but today digs are protected by laws that reserve the right to claim such treasures as national property.

EGYPTIAN FINDS

In 1996 Franck Goddio and his team discovered the lost island of Antirhodos, near the Egyptian city of Alexandria, where the last pharaoh, Cleopatra (69–30 B.C.E), ruled. Large parts of Alexandria

▲ The *Titanic*, which sank in the North Atlantic in 1912, was found, explored, and photographed in 1985.

were destroyed by earthquakes and tidal waves in the 500s C.E. Goddio's team revealed the layout and construction of the Royal Quarter of the ancient city and retrieved many artifacts. Archaeological investigations will continue in this historically important place. These will concentrate not just on ancient Egyptian remains, but also on Napoleonic warships wrecked there in the Battle of the Nile in the late 18th century. ◆

▲ A remotely operated vehicle (ROV) inspects a wreck. This is just one of many inventions at archaeologists' disposal today.

FACT FILE

Cleopatra's Palace
More than 2,000 years old. Found in 1996 by Franck Goddio and his team. In an effort to uncover ancient artifacts beneath the silt of Alexandria's harbor, they uncovered the lost island of Antirhodos (where the palace was built) and much of Alexandria's Royal Quarter

Finds
Statues of Great Priestess Isis and Mark Antony; two sphinxes; granite bust of Roman Emperor Augustus; remains of a pier from the 5th century B.C.E.; shipwreck from 90 B.C.E. – 130 C.E.

ARCHERFISH

Archerfish are grouped in the small family Toxotidae (tahk-SUH-tih-dee), which contains just six species found in coastal marine or brackish waters. *Toxotes jaculator* is one of the most widespread species of archerfish: its range extends from India through the Philippines and Australia to Polynesia. Archerfish generally inhabit muddy, brackish waters near mangroves and river mouths, although some species occur in freshwater.

APPEARANCE

Archerfish vary in color, depending on their distribution. For example, young individuals from Southeast Asia tend to be yellow-green to brown on their back, with their sides a delicate grayish green, gradually changing to a whitish silver underneath. Some archerfish have dark round marks or broad black bars extending across the body. These markings are most common in young-sters and begin to disappear as the fish get older, when they are restricted to the upper half of the body. Young archerfish live in groups, and bright yellow reflective flecks near the middle of their back help them maintain contact with each other. Older fish, which tend to be solitary, do not have these shiny flecks.

Archerfish are usually less than 6 inches (15 cm) long, but one species (*Toxotes chatareus*) reaches a length of 16 inches (41 cm). These fish have a triangular body, flattened from side to side, with their dorsal and anal fins set far back. This shape allows them to cruise

undetected just below the surface of the water, looking out for unsuspecting prey in the vegetation above.

SHOOT TO KILL

Archerfish particularly like to feed on insects such as cockroaches, crickets,

▼ Although they usually shoot insects down with a jet of water, archerfish will also leap vigorously from the water to catch their prey.

◀ **An archerfish shoots droplets of water at high speed from its mouth to knock insects off overhanging branches and into the water.**

on leaves and twigs above the water's surface with a powerful jet of water that they spout from their mouth. This is why they have been given the common name archerfish. Adults are able to target prey up to 5 feet (1.5 m) above them. If the first shot fails, they squirt several others in rapid succession.

Archerfish shoot water by powerfully contracting their gill covers and expelling the water through a tube formed by the tongue and a groove on the roof of the mouth. The aim is regulated using the thin tip of the tongue. Young fish, measuring just 1 inch (2.5 cm) long, can spout small drops of water, though these barely reach 4 inches (10 cm) into the air. Continuous practice makes them highly skilled by the time they have matured into adults.

Archerfish also possess excellent binocular vision, which enables them to judge distances accurately. In addition to this, when they aim the jet of water at their prey, they allow for the fact that light bends as it passes from the air to the water. ◆

grasshoppers, and flies; but they also eat a wide variety of aquatic organisms, including small crustaceans.

The most striking feature of archerfish is the way they hunt their prey: these fish shoot down insects crawling about

FACT FILE

Name
Archerfish
(*Toxotes jaculator*)

Distinctive features
Large eyes; dorsal and caudal fins yellow-green; dorsal and anal fins set well back on body; anal fin silvery with black edge; young have marked black bands that run up and down body

Habitat
Brackish waters, such as estuaries and swamps in Indo-Pacific

Behavior
Adults solitary; young form groups

Food
Mainly insects

Breeding
Breeding habits are not very well known; sexually mature when 4 in (10 cm) long

Lifespan
About 10 years

Size
Up to 10 in (25 cm) long

SEE ALSO

• Estuary
• Fish
• Insect
• Mangrove swamp

WHERE IN THE WORLD

Toxotes jaculator
Surface waters

Toxotes chatareus
Surface waters

ARCTIC OCEAN

The Arctic Ocean is the smallest of the world's oceans—some scientists even consider it to be part of the Atlantic. The North Pole is located close to the center of the Arctic. Almost completely surrounded by land, the ocean opens to the Pacific through the narrow Bering Strait, between Alaska and Siberia and to the Atlantic through the slightly larger Fram Strait between Greenland and Norway. Its area is 5,440,000 square miles (14,090,000 sq km), which is only one-tenth the size of the Pacific Ocean.

ICE CAPPED

At first glance, the Arctic may not seem like an ocean at all. Ice and snow cover the top of Earth almost completely. Around 60 percent of the surface is covered in ice even during the summer, while 90 percent is solid in winter. The surface ice sheet is between 6 and 12 feet (2 and 4 m) thick. Even the long summer days are not able to melt all this ice.

▲ Walruses haul out on the ice to breed. In spring, walruses are found only in the Arctic, but they migrate to warmer waters in the fall.

BENEATH THE ICE CAP

Wind, tides, and currents move the Arctic ice cap. A portion of the sea ice forms and melts each year, while another part remains as a more permanent ice cap. As sea ice forms, the salt is expelled as brine. After one year, enough salt has been removed for the ice to be melted and used as drinking water. The older ice is pale blue and is very hard. It is called polar pack.

As the ice moves it may break apart or be pushed together to create long raised features called pressure ridges. When the ice breaks apart, in areas called leads, great cracks of open water appear. These allow Arctic animals, such as seals and whales, to rise to the surface to breathe. The people of the

▲ In September and October one of the first signs that winter is coming is the formation of pancake ice: thin plates of ice that cover the water's surface like water lilies on a pond.

FACT FILE

Arctic Ocean
The world's smallest ocean

Climate
Temperatures average 32°F (0°C) in July and from −22°F to −40°F (−30°C to −40°C) in January; less than 10 in (25 cm) rainfall per year

Wildlife
Microscopic algae, fish, krill; seals, walruses, whales; polar bears live on the ice and hunt seals

Threats
Overfishing, pollution, global warming

Arctic understand the movements of the ice and are careful when they travel or hunt for food on its surface.

UNDER THE CAP

The Arctic Ocean probably formed around 66 million years ago, although it may not always have been covered by ice as it is today. A section of the mid-ocean ridge runs through the Arctic, separating the two relatively shallow basins that make up the seafloor. The maximum depth of the ocean is 18,050 feet (5,502 m), and the average depth is 3,240 feet (990 m).

Around the basins are extensions of the land called continental shelves. Rich in nutrients, these shallows support large numbers of creatures in the summer. Migrating whales and seals go through the narrow Bering Strait to reach these feeding grounds. For thousands of years, the people of Alaska and Siberia have hunted these animals. Although whaling is now banned, some Arctic communities are still permitted to hunt whales in limited numbers.

POLLUTION

A few rivers deposit freshwater and sediment into the waters of the Arctic.

This has enriched the shallow coastal edges of the ocean with extra nutrients. Today the area is threatened by pollution, particularly from Russian rivers, which carry waste from oil fields and nuclear dumps. While very few people actually live on the Arctic ice, pollution from other parts of the world threatens what was once a place of pure white snow and ice. ◆

▲ **Killer whales are a common sight in the Arctic Ocean. They are sociable animals that live in groups called pods of up to 20 whales. The members of a pod communicate with each other and co-operate in hunting fish, squid, sea lions, seals, and even other whales and dolphins.**

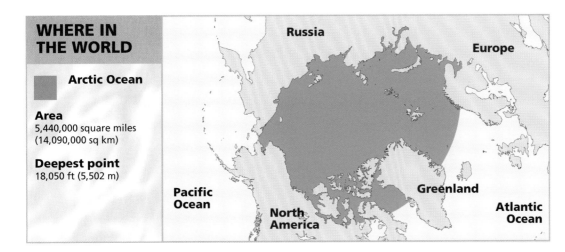

WHERE IN THE WORLD

Arctic Ocean

Area
5,440,000 square miles
(14,090,000 sq km)

Deepest point
18,050 ft (5,502 m)

Russia

Europe

Pacific Ocean

North America

Greenland

Atlantic Ocean

SEE ALSO

- Antarctic Ocean
- Atlantic Ocean
- Global warming
- Iceberg
- Killer whale
- Pacific Ocean
- Polar bear

ATLANTIC OCEAN

The ancient Greeks named the Atlantic, or the Sea of Atlas, after the mythological figure who carries the world on his shoulders. The Atlantic is the second largest ocean. It covers almost 20 percent of Earth's surface, an area of 41,100,000 square miles (106,460,000 sq km). Its average depth is 12,877 feet (3,926 m), and the deepest spot is in the Puerto Rico Trench, where the seabed descends 27,493 feet (8,380 m) below the surface.

The Atlantic extends south to Antarctica and includes several smaller seas around its margins. The North Sea, the Mediterranean Sea, the Caribbean Sea, and the Gulf of Mexico are among the marginal seas of the Atlantic; they are separated from it by land extensions or island chains. The Atlantic has relatively few oceanic islands, although among them is the world's largest island, Greenland. Many of the islands around its margins, such as the British Isles, are parts of the continental landmasses that have become separated from the continents by erosion.

NEWLY FORMED

The Atlantic Ocean is growing as the continents of Europe and Africa drift away from North and South America. The bottom of the Atlantic is spreading out from the Mid-Atlantic Ridge, an

▲ **This relief map of the globe shows the Mid-Atlantic Ridge as a lighter blue line that runs through the center of the ocean. Despite being up to 1.5 miles (2.5 km) below sea level, the ridge is home to a diversity of life-forms. Bacteria, worms, crabs, fish, and shrimp, adapted to life in the dark cold waters, flourish around scalding-hot hydrothermal vents.**

WHERE IN THE WORLD

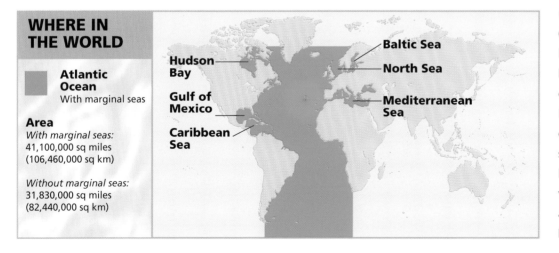

■ **Atlantic Ocean**
With marginal seas

Area
With marginal seas:
41,100,000 sq miles
(106,460,000 sq km)

Without marginal seas:
31,830,000 sq miles
(82,440,000 sq km)

Hudson Bay

Gulf of Mexico

Caribbean Sea

Baltic Sea

North Sea

Mediterranean Sea

underwater mountain range that splits the ocean into two basins. The ridge extends for more than 10,000 miles (16,000 km) from Iceland almost to Antarctica, and it is up to 1,000 miles (1,600 km) wide in places. Molten rock emerges from beneath Earth's crust along the ridge and hardens to form new seabed. The process began around 180 million years ago when the continents first broke apart. In a few places the peaks of the Mid-Atlantic Ridge break the surface to form islands. Elsewhere, volcanic islands such as Bermuda and the Azores also rise steeply from the ocean floor.

EROSION FROM LAND

Large parts of the continents that border the Atlantic (North America, South America, Europe, and Africa) slope toward the ocean. The land therefore drains huge amounts of freshwater and sediment onto the ocean floor. The sediments (silt, dust, and runoff from land) lie along the edges of the continents and build up in deposits that can be 10,000 to 50,000 feet (3,000 to 15,000 m) thick. Over millions of years some of the world's largest deposits of petroleum, natural gas, and coal have built up within these sediments.

In North America the mighty Mississippi River, the Saint Lawrence River, and a large number of smaller rivers all flow into the Atlantic. In South America the world's largest river, the Amazon, flows east into the Atlantic, emptying along the coast of Brazil. In Africa the Congo River flows west to empty into the opposite side of the ocean. The Orinoco, the Niger, and many of Europe's famous rivers carry water, sediments, and sometimes pollution into the Atlantic.

RIVER IN THE OCEAN

In the Atlantic itself, another "river" flows, stronger and longer even than the Amazon. Known as the Gulf Stream, it is one of the many currents that move the waters of all oceans around the world.

FACT FILE

Atlantic Ocean
The second largest and the youngest ocean

Habitats
A wide range of tropical, polar, and temperate marine habitats, including kelp forests, coral reefs, estuaries, brine pools, and hydrothermal vents

Threats
Hurricanes; overfishing of fish such as the Atlantic cod; pollution, especially along busy shipping routes and near large population centers, industrial complexes, and around estuaries

◄ Tube anemones are common in sandy bottoms on the continental shelf in the North Atlantic. Unlike true sea anemones, these animals do not attach to rocks but dig their columns into the sediments. They can retract very quickly into these tubes. Other animals, such as redfish, use the tubes for shelter.

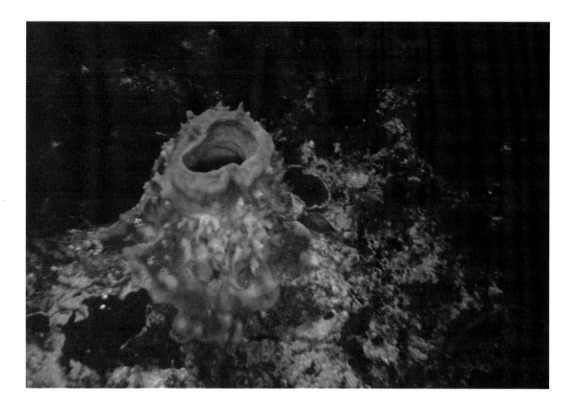

◀ Impressive coral reefs mark the divide between the main body of the Atlantic Ocean and the Gulf of Mexico, one of its marginal seas. These reefs have developed around a chain of volcanic islands and are home to a huge variety of organisms, including sponges (like the one shown here on a deep reef), corals, snails, jellyfish, sea anemones, crabs, lobsters, fish, and sea turtles.

Surface currents are the best known, but whenever water moves away from one area, water must move into that area to replace it. Therefore, deep ocean currents often flow in the opposite direction to surface ones. The Gulf Stream behaves like a river because it tends to stay within bounds. The banks are not of earth, but of colder and denser water. The Gulf Stream can actually be seen as a different color than the ocean water around it. Ocean water tends to circulate clockwise north of the equator and counterclockwise south of it in all the ocean basins, due to the prevailing winds and the rotation of Earth.

The Gulf Stream is one of the most defined of the surface currents. It builds up as prevailing winds blow westward along the equator. The water flows into the Caribbean Sea and into the Gulf of Mexico and then northward before moving eastward as the Gulf Stream and heading toward northern Europe.

The warm water of the Gulf Stream changes the weather all along the Atlantic coast and warms the British Isles more than their northern location would otherwise allow. The Gulf Stream also brings tropical fishes as far north as Cape Cod in the summer and allows the island of Bermuda to be home to the same butterfly fish and angelfish that are found in waters much farther south.

THE SARGASSO SEA

In the center of the currents that circulate around the North Atlantic, a relatively calm area exists. This is called the Sargasso Sea. While it is not bounded by land, it is defined by the pattern of circulation around it. This is the breeding ground for the American and European eels. Young eels, tiny leaflike creatures, hatch there and are then carried along the Gulf Stream to find, in ways that are yet to be completely understood, a home river in

FACT FILE

Climate
In the North Atlantic between spring and fall, regular cyclonic storms pass east along the border where cold air from polar regions meets mild air from the Tropics. Farther south, a high-pressure belt between 15 and 30°N mostly lacks bad storms. In the South Atlantic similar weather patterns occur in the Australian winter, with westerlies known as roaring forties, and a calmer high-pressure zone to the north

which they will grow for several years. On reaching maturity, the adults return to the Sargasso Sea to spawn.

FISHERIES

Since times long before the Europeans reached North America, the Atlantic has been feeding the coastal populations around its shores. As the New World developed, new fisheries extended farther out to sea. Cod, haddock, hake, herring, and mackerel were found in enormous schools in the waters over shallow continental shelves, called banks. For example, Grand Bank off Newfoundland, Georges Bank off Cape Cod, and the banks of the North Sea have been fished for centuries. Many of the fish populations targeted there are now in serious decline.

Cod stocks, which helped make the newly formed United States a rich nation, are now a fraction of the original, and the haddock are all but gone. Controls have been placed on these fish-eries in the hope of saving the stocks that are left. However, controls such as these can only be effective if they are enforced, and constant monitoring is required to ensure that fish stocks that are currently not listed as threatened do not come to be so. ◆

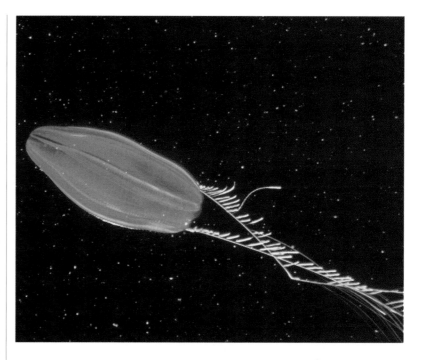

▲ A sea gooseberry, a type of comb jelly, drifts in the Atlantic. The long tentacles are used to capture tiny organisms of the plankton.

◄ Soldier fish are widespread in tropical waters in the Atlantic. They are found close to reefs, to rocky shores, and in caves. These nocturnal fish make a variety of grunts and squeaks.

SEE ALSO
• Antarctic Ocean
• Gulf of Mexico
• Mediterranean Sea
• Midocean ridge

BACTERIA

◄ These stromatolites, pictured in Sharks Bay, Australia, are cyanobacterial mats layered with sediment. Such structures are known to have formed as far back as 3.5 billion years ago.

FACT FILE

Extremophilic bacteria
Live in environments with extreme conditions, such as acidic or hot springs, salt lakes, hydrothermal vents, ice

Thermophilic bacteria
Extremophiles that live in very hot water environments, such as in hot springs and around hydrothermal vents; they thrive on chemicals in the hot waters

Bacteria are the simplest and smallest forms of life. Viruses are smaller, but they are not technically alive and must enter other living cells before they can reproduce. Bacteria are single cells, and many are tiny, averaging just one micrometer (a millionth of a meter) in diameter. They differ from other living organisms in that they do not have a discrete nucleus that contains their genetic material. Instead, their DNA occurs in a loose mass called the nuclear body. Also present are small loops of free-floating DNA, called plasmids, that can be transmitted to other bacteria.

Bacteria are constructed on a very simple plan, without the internal structures found in cells of higher animals and plants. They may be shaped like small spheres, rods, threads, or strings of beads. Some forms have hairlike pili,

which they use to stick themselves to surfaces, and one or more whiplike flagella, which they beat to propel themselves. When faced with poor living conditions, most bacteria produce tough, resistant spores that lie dormant for a long time—up to 3,000 years—before coming back to life. Bacteria reproduce by splitting into two identical cells or by budding off small cells.

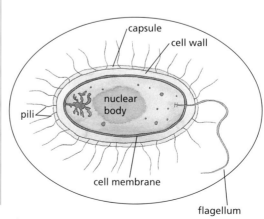

◄ A generalized diagram of a bacterium, showing typical features. Not all bacteria have every feature.

BACTERIAL ENVIRONMENTS

Bacteria are found in most environments, even where no other living organisms can survive. They feed on almost any organic material and even some unlikely substances, such as metals and sulfur. Almost all solid underwater surfaces are covered with a material called a biofilm, which is made up of bacteria in a sticky mass of mucus. The mucus sticks the bacteria to the surface, helps them control their environment, and prevents them from being attacked by other microorganisms.

Some bacteria are parasitic, living inside other organisms and sometimes causing disease. For example, the bacterium *Escherichia coli* causes disease in humans when it is swallowed; it can be found in water and on unwashed fruits and vegetables contaminated by sewage. Other bacteria cause serious diseases such as typhoid and cholera.

AQUATIC SCAVENGERS

Bacteria fall into two main groups: autotrophs, which make their own food; and heterotrophs, which consume other microorganisms or organic particles. Heterotrophic bacteria are either aerobic, which means they need oxygen to survive, or anaerobic. Anaerobic bacteria do not need oxygen to live and can actually be poisoned by it. These anaerobic bacteria live in huge numbers in soils and in sediments. In the process of breaking down organic matter for food, they produce foul-smelling hydrogen sulfide gas.

EXTREME CONDITIONS

One of the most extreme environments inhabited by bacteria is hot mineral springs, where these microorganisms

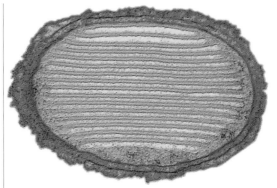

sometimes exist at temperatures of 212°F (100°C) or more. In hot mineral springs, mats of cyanobacteria, or blue-green algae, build up layers that become mineralized, generally with silica. Such organisms are thought to be some of the oldest forms of life.

Bacteria have also been found living around underwater hot springs, called hydrothermal vents, in the ocean depths. Here bacteria are known to live at temperatures that reach 248°F (120°C), and some scientists think they have found bacteria that live at temperatures of almost 392°F (200°C). Specialized forms of bacteria inhabit the seas of the Antarctic and even the Dead Sea, where the salt concentration is so high that nothing else can survive. ◆

◄ This extremophilic bacterium lives in hot pools, where it finds the high levels of dissolved chemicals that it needs to survive.

SEE ALSO

- Algae
- Amoeba
- Bioluminescence
- Hydrothermal vent

▼ Cyanobacteria grow in large matlike communities in still water. They need to live close to the surface to have access to sunlight for photosynthesis. Too many cyanobacteria can deplete waters of oxygen, killing fish and other animals.

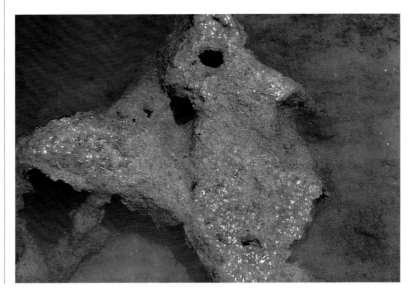

BARNACLE

Barnacles are crustaceans, but for many years they were considered to be mollusks because they have a protective shell made of calcium carbonate just like clams and oysters do. The relationship of barnacles to other crustaceans is not obvious, except in the larvae (young forms), which resemble small shrimp.

The barnacle's shell is made of tough plates of calcium carbonate, which surround the body and protect it from the waves and predators. Most species of coastal barnacles are small, but some deep-water barnacles reach a length of 30 inches (76 cm).

Although all crustaceans have the same basic body plan, each species is adapted to suit its way of life, and barnacles are among the most highly modified crustaceans. Barnacles are the only crustaceans that are unable to move around as adults. They can be found in marine and estuarine environments, along the seashore

and attached to pilings; in deeper waters they attach to a wide range of firm surfaces, from rocks and ships to whales. Many are exposed at low tide, and they can feed only when the water covers them. Others, however, live so high up in the tidal zone that they are never fully submerged. Barnacles can withstand desiccation (drying out) for periods of time—they trap water inside their shell and close it tight—but they must spend some time underwater in order to feed.

FEEDING

Barnacles have been called animals that stand on their heads and kick food into their mouths, and that is an accurate description. Their "head" is firmly attached to a solid surface by what would be the antennae in other forms of crustaceans. Barnacles have six pairs of appendages, or legs, called cirri, which are edged with fine bristles. When the barnacle

▲ A lengthwise section of a goose barnacle. The animal produces both sperm (from the male sex organ) and eggs (from the female ovary) but cannot self-fertilize. Like other crustaceans, barnacles molt, shedding their body's thin hard covering, the exoskeleton. This is not the shell, which is never shed.

◄ Barnacles can attach to many solid surfaces, including a sea turtle's shell, whales, and pilings. Some barnacles attach to jellyfish. These barnacles are not parasites, as they do not feed on the animal's tissues.

SEE ALSO

- Crustacean
- Parasite

▶ Two acorn barnacles, just visible amid a mass of sea anemones, extend their cirri to feed. If a shadow passes over the barnacle, the cirri will be quickly pulled inside the shell. This protects the cirri from being eaten by a passing fish.

FACT FILE

Name
Acorn barnacles (*Balanus* species)

Distinctive features
Whitish, volcano-shaped shell attached to firm surface; six pairs of cirri; no stalk (peduncle)

Habitat
Rocks and pilings of intertidal zone

Food
Plankton via filter feeding

Breeding
Although acorn barnacles mate, fertilization occurs outside the body but inside the shell

Lifespan
Not known

Size
Less than 1 in (2.5 cm) across

feeds, blood is pumped into the cirri, causing them to unroll into a fan shape. The outstretched cirri are swept back and forth two or three times a second, trapping small floating organisms like a net. Once caught, the food is passed down into the mouth. If the barnacle is alarmed, the cirri are snatched back into the shell by powerful muscles. Two pairs of the shell plates can close off the opening through which the appendages protrude, sealing the barnacle in and preventing it from drying out when exposed at low tide.

TYPES OF BARNACLES

Barnacles fall into three main groups. Acorn barnacles attach directly to a solid surface, while goose, or stalked, barnacles are attached by a long leathery stalk called a peduncle. The peduncles of some species of goose barnacles are eaten by humans. Parasitical barnacles live on other marine organisms or bore into coral or the shells of mollusks.

REPRODUCTION

Most barnacles are hemaphrodites, which means that they have male and female sex organs. They still need to mate, however, as the sperm of one barnacle cannot fertilize the same barnacle's eggs. Most barnacles brood their fertilized eggs outside their body but inside their shell until the larvae hatch. The larvae are very similar to those of other crustaceans. After passing through several developmental stages while floating in the plankton, the larva attaches itself by its head to a solid surface, using a kind of cement secreted from the base of its antennae. It then builds the plates of its shell and turns into an adult. ◆

▶ To reproduce, an acorn barnacle inserts its long male sex organ into the shell of another, delivering sperm to fertilize its neighbor's eggs.

BARRACUDA

There are around 20 different species of barracuda, all belonging to the family Sphyraenidae (sfie-REE-nih-dee). The name of the family comes from the Greek word for hammer, because the head of the fish is shaped like the hammer used by geologists when they are collecting rocks and fossils. Barracuda are found in all the world's tropical oceans, and some range into temperate seas as well.

LARGE, FAST FISH

The barracuda's body is green to steel gray above, silvery with a yellow band along the side, and whitish below. The sides of most species also have dark bands or inky blotches. Barracuda in the wild can reach lengths of 4 to 6 feet (1.2 to 1.8 m) and weigh up to 100 pounds (45 kg). The great barracuda of the Caribbean Sea and Pacific Ocean is the largest species. Reports from the 18th century describe barracudas that were nearly 20 feet (6 m) long. The official record for the largest barracuda to be caught, however, is for a fish that was only 5½ feet (1.7 m) long.

Barracuda are long and slender with a pointed head. They have two dorsal fins, widely separated from each other, and the tail is forked. Shaped like a torpedo, barracuda can move very quickly through the water. However,

▲ Barracuda are generally solitary animals, though the Pacific barracuda can be found in small schools in shallow inshore waters. Large schools of spawning great barracuda have been observed, and some barracuda attack schools of prey at the same time, scattering their victims and making individuals easier to catch.

60

although they can reach speeds of up to 27 miles per hour (43 km/h) in short bursts, they do not have the stamina to sustain fast swimming for long periods.

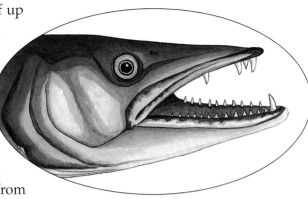

◄ The barracuda's sharp inward-pointing teeth are nearly always reserved for grasping fish and squid; attacks on humans are rare. They make one fierce strike that is rarely fatal.

LIFE CYCLE

Barracuda can live for 30 years, but few individuals survive this long. The average lifespans are from 11 to 14 years, depending on the species. Barracuda breed from April to October, and they gather in large schools to spawn. Fertilized eggs float in the open ocean, unprotected by the adults. Young barracuda prefer sandy and weedy shallows, where they feed largely on fish such as gobies, mojarras, atherinids, young parrot fish, and needlefish. When they reach a length of about 2 feet (60 cm), however, they change their habitat and diet. Adults live in a wide range of habitats but are mostly offshore or on coral reefs, where they eat different species of fish, such as snappers, grunts, pufferfish, jacks, sea bass, halfbeaks, and mackerel.

BAD REPUTATION?

Barracuda are voracious carnivores, feeding mainly on fish, although they also feed on shrimp and cephalopods, such as squid and cuttlefish. Great barracuda have a reputation for being fierce and dangerous to humans. The generally smaller Pacific barracuda is not considered to be a threat to humans at all. Although more than 30 attacks by barracuda on humans have occurred in the Caribbean, this reputation is largely undeserved because attacks are relatively rare. Their bad reputation is probably partly based on the fish's fearsome appearance: barracuda have staring eyes and a formidable array of very long, sharp teeth, which hook inward slightly. The teeth are all the more noticeable because of the large, forward-projecting mouth. Barracuda do not seem to be particularly aggressive or territorial in their behavior,

FACT FILE

Name
Great barracuda
(*Sphyraena barracuda*)

Distinctive features
Torpedo-shaped body, with long, thin jaws; scattered black blotches on sides; green to steel gray on back; whitish belly

Habitat
Juveniles live in mangroves; estuaries; shallow, sheltered inner reef areas. Adults range widely, from harbors to the open sea

Behavior
Day swimming; usually solitary

Food
Mainly fish, squid, and octopuses but also shrimp

Lifespan
Up to 30 years

Size
Up to 5½ ft (1.7 m) long and 100 lb (45 kg)

WHERE IN THE WORLD

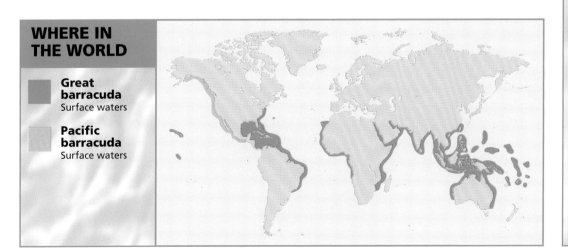

Great barracuda
Surface waters

Pacific barracuda
Surface waters

however, except during the breeding season. When barracuda do attack humans, it is usually by mistake. These fish are bold and inquisitive, and they attack anything moving in the water in a way that could be mistaken for another fish in trouble. The risk to humans seems to be greater when only a part of the body is submerged or when people are swimming in muddy water, so the barracuda cannot make out their shape clearly. To avoid attack from barracuda, bathers should not carry fish in the water or wear shiny jewelry.

POISONOUS FLESH

For sport fishers, barracuda make good game fish: they fight well and when hooked in shallow waters they make incredibly swift runs and frequent spectacular jumps. The flesh in many large individuals can be poisonous to humans, however. This is because of their diet of coral reef-grazing fish. Some corals contain tiny algae that produce a poison called ciguatera. Reef-grazing fish such as surgeonfish and parrot fish consume these algae and so become toxic themselves. The poison becomes concentrated in the flesh of larger carnivorous fish that catch and eat many of these grazers.

It is estimated that every year around 20,000 to 50,000 people suffer from poisoning when they eat fish contaminated with ciguatera. The symptoms are intense itching, headaches, and dizziness in the first 2 to 12 hours after eating the poison, and in some rare cases death results. The great barracuda is one of the prime agents of ciguatera poisoning in the Caribbean. ◆

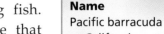

FACT FILE

Name
Pacific barracuda or California barracuda (*Sphyraena argentea*)

Habitat
Shallow inshore waters, estuaries, and bays

Breeding
All adults can breed by the age of 3. Season: April to September

Food
Smaller fish

Lifespan
Up to 20 years

Size
Up to 4 ft (1.2 m)

◀ Great barracuda are frequently encountered near reefs in the Caribbean. They are very curious fish and will sometimes follow closely behind divers. Although capable of rapid bursts of speed to catch prey, most of the time they swim slowly in the water.

SEE ALSO

• Caribbean Sea
• Coral reef
• Fish
• Locomotion
• Reproduction

GLOSSARY

antennae: protruding "feelers" or sense organs common in invertebrates; used to touch, smell, hear, and taste the surroundings

buoyancy: the force of the water surrounding a floating object that prevents it from sinking

camouflage: coloring or texture of an organism's outer covering that makes it look like its surroundings; used to hide from predators and prey

carbohydrate: a type of food that includes sugar, starch, and fiber

carnivores: animals (and a few plants) that eat other animals

calcium carbonate: a white chemical used in bones, shells, and carapaces; it is also found in limestone, chalk, and marble

cilia: tiny hairlike structures on the surface of cells used for feeding and locomotion

clutch: a collection of fertilized eggs laid at the same time by one mother

colonizing: when organisms of one or several species move into a previously unoccupied habitat

drag: a force that acts to slow down a body as it moves through water or air

ecosystem: a community of organisms of many species that are interdependent for survival

egg: female sex cell that, when fertilized by sperm, grows into a new individual

environment: the combination of plants and animals, chemicals, landscape, and climate in which an organism lives; also used to mean *nature*

enzyme: a protein usually used inside the body to manufacture substances needed for life

fertilization: the fusion of a sperm (male sex cell) and egg (female sex cell) to produce a single cell that will grow into a unique individual. Internal fertilization occurs inside the body; external fertilization occurs outside the body

fin: limblike extensions on fish used for propulsion and steering, but also for other specializations; fish may have different numbers of fins

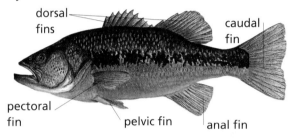

dorsal fins

caudal fin

pectoral fin

pelvic fin

anal fin

foot: the muscular part of a mollusk used mainly for movement or feeding

gills: organs used by aquatic animals to extract oxygen from water

habitat: the environment in which an organism is best suited to live

invertebrate: an animal without a backbone

larvae: young, immature animals, often very different from the adult form

mantle: the outer tissue of a mollusk from which the shell is secreted and attached to

medusa: free-floating stage in the life cycle of cnidarians such as jellyfish

metamorphosis: the process by which larvae turn into adults; may involve many small stages or a single major change

photosynthesis: the process by which organisms such as plants make sugar using sunlight

plankton: organisms that float in ocean currents

polyp: stage in the life cycle of cnidarians such as sea anemones; usually attached to a surface

pseudopod: an extension of a cell membrane, used mainly for movement and feeding by single-celled organisms and simple animals

sediment: substances that are deposited on a seabed; over time these sediments become rocks

vertebrate: an animal with a backbone

INDEX

Page numbers in *italics* refer to picture captions.